TINY MAD IDEA

The Relative World Belief - I

Sharon Moriarty, M.S.E.E.

GATEWAY TO ETERNITY PUBLICATIONS

http://www.GatewayToEternity.com

TINY MAD IDEA

ALL ABOARD THE TITANIC

There was this single thought percolating in my head for quite a while. Like some psychological virus, it had weaseled its way in, to hijack the entire process of my thought. Sure other thoughts would come and go, but this one always seemed to hang around. The thought was simply this. **"There is something fundamentally wrong with the world we live in."** What a lame and puerile thought it was on the surface, yet it pointed to an underlying veracity, I could no longer ignore.

Sure! Most know how the game of life is played. For the majority, it is one of maximizing happiness while minimizing effort and pain. A continual ego quest of gaining notoriety, wealth, and fame by the path of least resistance. A perpetual hunt for extracting pleasure, indulging various obsessions and occasionally doing a good deed or two, to assuage the demon of inner guilt. For some, it is also a pursuit of seducing any witless victim that crosses their path and engaging in petty power plays to gain dominance and control.

Every moment, we are bombarded by a million different novel solutions designed specifically to cater to all our physical and psychological needs. Some increase our sense of complacency, confidence and provide the illusion of security. Others immerse us in the virtual worlds of distractive entertainment, modern technology, and sense-orientated pleasures. A number inflate our self-worth and conceit so that we can continue to bit-blast our hot-air opinions and provocative tweets all around the world. It is evident that there are innumerable ingenious remedies, quick-fixes, magical cures and pills aimed at keeping us oversexed, tuned-out and basking in neurochemical laced ease.

We all live in a world, in which any trace of frustration or uncertainty is instantly rectifiable by legions of financial experts, legal advisors, priests, social counselors and spiritual gurus. All ready to answer the call and pander to our quandaries. Alternatively, we could just solicit any needed information from some social media site. However, the ultimate end-purpose and meaning of it all still seemed very vague and elusive to me. Were we just on an arbitrary joyride, in which we bartered and schemed for transient thrills and gratifications until the bucket finally tipped over?

A far more revealing question would be in asking, *"Why were we all hovering about here in bodies, in the first place?"* – bodies that would eventually fail or become worn out.

Why were we being presented with such a chaotic world of a gazillion meaningless objects? One in which there was so much anxiety, disorder, meanness, deception, and strife. A veritable zoo of crazed animals with all their pet addictions, drugs, and foolish fantasies. Why did we spend the greater part of our lives performing a plethora of purposeless tasks, just to eke out a morsel or two of real living?

Yes, there was no denying it. Most assuredly, there was an elephant in this room which we were conveniently ignoring. A giant gaping hole in the boat of existence that could never quite be patched. External solutions were bringing us nowhere. Instead, the insanity was growing asymptotically by the day, and we were heading fast towards the stratosphere of our doom. Like the Titanic, we would eventually go down. It was a metaphysical certainty because we were fighting a losing battle in a vengeful hall of mirrors and predestined to wear ourselves out. The endless array of peace accords, non-discrimination policies, political, social and economic initiatives all just functioned as more lipstick on the pig. It was all part of an invisible conspiracy to keep us sold on a dream of progress.

In the final analysis, it made no difference how many new toys we designed, or creature comforts we unleashed – all was part of a massive cover-up – a lid over a great stinking garbage bin! No amount of progress, effort or ingenuity could ever penetrate deeply enough, to heal us at our core. No invention or intervention could ever rescue us from what was shattered within. We were all biochemical Pinocchios, forever missing that critical ingredient, which could have made us real. Sure there were times, when I like everyone else, found myself floating about on the wings of bliss. Still, the next moment, I would come crashing back to Earth or even drop a little further into all the sewers and gutters of the world. I was always feeling like some tragic Dantesque figure on an alien planet, I did not know, or care to penetrate.

Despite all the illusory perks the world offered, the daggers were coming for us all. Soon the thorns would dig in deeper and cripple our every move. It was incontestable that the essential backdrop of the world was one of abiding misery. Hence all our frantic activities and foolish obsessions. All was just a convenient screen designed to shield us from the countless mindless cruelties and barbaric acts; we could never quite integrate. Yes, every joy was fleeting, and every success and accolade became tarnished all too soon. Thus, every celebrity would get to have their DUI mugshot and be torn apart wing-for-wing!

As for the rest of us, we were mere machines, joyless unknown citizens feeding the profiteering monsters and
brain-farms, popping up all around us. Machines, soon to
become outdated and obsolete, then relegated to the recy-
cling landfills and manure pastures that speckle our great
luniverse. With every passing year, we would find ourselves increasingly denuded of acumen, energy, acuity and
strength. Quenched of all enthusiasm and motivation. It
was only a matter of time before our adventurous spirits
would be mercilessly crushed into dust.

Next year's model would be a shabby, frosty, wrinkled hol-
lowed-out carcass. A demented figure stripped of all former glory. An aimless caricature in a meaningless dream,
that was entirely circumvented and vitiated of life. Yes,
soon we would all turn into scarecrows before our very
eyes. Scarecrows, only too happy to jump into our own
graves with glee. There seemed to be no inspired hope or
guaranteed trajectory offered by the world, by which to be
lastingly redeemed. As in the movie, 'Logan's Run,' there
was to be no outside chance of renewal. Instead, all were
to be expeditiously vaporized and scattered into the icy
cosmos.

**Or was there an alternative solution, temporarily lost
to my awareness?** Hence each day, I meditated intensely

on this question until I could feel it tearing me apart within. Even so, it all felt like some Zen Koan or Gordian knot that could never be unraveled in the context it was set.

ENCOUNTERING THE VOICE

T hen one day, an inner Voice spoke with a clarity and authority that was refreshing to hear. His first words were "*It is impossible to find any lasting happiness in the relative world, anymore than a fool, who thinks he has fallen into a mirror can extract life from the tenebrous shadows; he perceives within it. For these shadows will always remain powerless to restore him to any true sanity or peace.*"

"I don't quite get the analogy," I quickly responded.

Then it spoke again, "*You too have fallen in a mirror and do not recognize it. This mirror is this world you see. Nevertheless, since you have never been here, it cannot give what you demand. For it has no more solidity or depth to it than a dream of the night. It remains an empty, superficial, lost world powered solely by your irrational thoughts. One shaped by all those arbitrary ideations emerging out of your desires and fears. Everywhere, its meaninglessness is evident. However, the extent of your denial is so immense that you can rarely admit to it. Since you fear this realization would ultimately destroy you, and bankrupt all hope, your anxiety is incessantly bubbling below the surface, getting ready to finally boil over.*

So you cling to numerous straws, which soon prove fruitless! All the same, where else but in a world of skin-deep fantasies, could the vain and self-absorbed thrive, while the purely motivated go hungry and be left to die? Where else but in a counterfeit shadowland of the shallowest proportions, could seedy tales of scandal and corruption take precedence over truth? Consequently, you witness a world consumed by various forms of sensationalism, undying streams of marketing fads, and numerous other chimerical apparitions of the mind. One in which, underlying intention does not seem to be of any importance. For it is a world built on a foundation of denial and self-deception from the start."

This Voice seemed to have some revelatory answers that I had never heard before. Reason told me, it could hardly have a twisted agenda since it was entirely bodiless. It was unlikely, therefore, to be poisoned and contaminated by impure self-serving motives, as most bodies are. All the same, I desired to cross-examine it, hoping to catch it in a snare or two. So I asked, "*Who Are You?*"

"*What Am I? is a more appropriate question,*" it swiftly declared. Then proceeded, "*I am the **Voice of Truth** and the **Voice of the One-Mind**. That all-knowing, laconic inner voice, whom you mask under a deluge of desires, worldly ambitions, and toxic thoughts. The gibberish ranting of your* *ego stifles and overwhelms me most of the time. So we must be prompt if you would listen to the wisdom I have to impart!"*

"What is your relationship to Jesus, the Buddha, Osho, Shankaracharya and other Enlightened Masters of the past?"

"As Truth is One, we are One! Do you conceive each liberated being maintains a separate existence, once they attain to Truth?"

"In that case, can you kindly put Jesus on the line? because I have a ton of questions to ask him!"

Since time seemed scarce, I skipped the ice-breaking introductions and immediately fired off with my first question.

"What exactly is the Relative World and why should I care a toss to learn more?"

GOING DOWN THE RABBIT HOLE

Then came Jesus's response, "**The Relative World is this world of your perceptions. Since nothing here is Absolute, nothing here is Real!** All appearances here depend on a profusion of other illusions to bolster and reinforce the mirage of their existence. The pseudo-reality of each derives from the copious comparisons, evaluations, and judgments, your mind makes, which help to distinguish each from a host of other illusions. Its entire basis of being is founded on the laws of contingency — not those of Truth! Even so, no appearance can stand on its own two feet. None can self-validate its individual existence. Once you probe deeply enough into its self-nature and essence, you find you are holding an empty picture. One depleted of all meaningful content, yet housed in an overly elaborate and glitzy frame. Each element of your perception attempts unceasingly to fool and bedazzle you with the most clever and quick-handed conjuring tricks. The web of chiaroscuro each spins in your mind is carefully woven from the imprisoning nexus of all your beliefs, desires, biases, predilections and prejudices. Once you go past all this, you find there is nothing at its core.

Worldly folk cannot recognize how they are being conned by these bogus magician tricks. So they commit to this world exclusively and believe it is all there is! They settle for a life of mediocrity inside the mirror and then immediately go about demanding a high return on all their investments. This pragmatic bartering strategy is only natural, because each seems to cost them directly in terms of time, effort, and lost opportunities. Soon they become very clinical and demanding in their approach – always seeking to glean and wangle more than they are willing to give.

Their outrageous and unrealistic demands of life and insatiable desires utterly consume them. Thus you see them scurrying about like frenzied, acephalic ants, lost to themselves while navigating about like mindless automatons in a dream. For there are always more bills to be paid, relationships to satisfy, adventures to experience, work to be done, pleasures to be indulged, debt collectors to avoid. So many joyless tasks, endlessly besieging them that compete for their full attention. The *important and non-urgent* rarely takes any precedence on the radar of their minds over the *unimportant but urgent*. Hence, this superficial world is the altar on which they sacrifice all their days until that portentous moment when it is finally too late. What most fail, to recognize is that their cold, calculating and extortionist approach to life costs them vision. For they fail to realize that they are always trading in illusions, spun from within — illusions that then cast a veil over the Real.

Their failure to be still, merely for an instant prevents the universe of Truth from pouring in to heal them. Even if they do stop momentarily, their minds are brimming with so many ambitious thoughts that Truth is powerless to penetrate beyond the mental mists. Their entire thinking approach is to self-justify and rationalize all their Machiavellian viewpoints. Interpreting the needs of others, as apart from their own, they spend all their time and resources undividedly on themselves. Ergo, just like that, the competition instinct kicks in fueling their endless rationalizations for failing to be altruistic and inclusive. So, while the poor, disabled and broken grovel near their feet, they endorse a life philosophy that caters exclusively to their personal interests.

If they had merely switched the dynamic from extortion and greed to one of blessing and sharing, they would have found their abundance. Spirit, being a limitless and inexhaustible powerhouse, would have given them, instantaneously everything they truly needed or desired. It would have taught them that this universe has always been nothing but a product of one's thoughts and that all true gifts are just a thought away!

Regrettably, their hard-boiled philistine approach to life severs all connection to spirit. All of which prevents them from accessing its fathomless wells of wisdom and inspiration and eventually leaves them vulnerable to all forms of mental and physical sickness. Since they foolishly conceive others are out to steal the various trinkets they have hoarded, they become riddled with tremendous fear and paranoia.

You asked, '**Why should I care a toss to learn more?**' So I ask, '**How are you feeling right now?**' Do you feel unconditionally loved, loving and cheerful at all times? Are you radiating peace and contentment? Do you feel valued, appreciated and indispensable? Is your life throbbing with meaning and your future positively glowing? Is it going to exceed all your expectations and blow your mind away? Or is there just a small hint of discontent present somewhere? A slight twinge of annoyance at the world at times — like when a fly lands on your nose when you are barreling down the highway, that will not bugger off? Is it not possible that you have lost some of the magic and mystery? Detected this game of charades is not real living? Maybe you have become a little wound down and bruised by life? Dispossessed of some of your former optimism, drive, and spirit of adventure?"

My mind was now cranking on all cylinders. It was as if Jesus knew how to read me from the inside-out. He certainly knew how to press all the right buttons. There seemed everything to be gained from being perfectly honest.

I quickly expressed my true feelings, "Mostly I feel like a great white shark, and duped into living out my life in a giant goldfish bowl. I see everywhere goldfish swimming about, wagging their tails in merriment. Pleased and enchanted by the most superficial things. They are like happy kids, who think everything is new. Only too ready then to overlook that cruel mixture of boredom, stress, anxiety, and sweat they pay to get the toys they want. At other times, I feel more like a stranger, isolated and abandoned in a hostile landscape. Despite all the tacky allurements and empty seductions, this world shovels daily into my face; I find my heart does not sing as it should. It is an overdressed universe powered by countless strange looking symbols, concepts, titles, tricks and evil maneuverings.

There seem to be too many wrappings of deception interposed between my living experience and what I crave the most. Nor have I reaped immense rewards, from the enormous investments, I have expended to date! I think implanting this hope of finding lasting happiness and peace here, is a mean trick. Just something to lure the suckers in and keep them moving like rats in a cage. At most, happiness comes in drips and spurts, and it is gone all too soon. Nor does this looney bin even seem capable of providing any illuminating answers to all questions of vital importance! Very few have figured out that there is a major piece missing in this jigsaw. Rather, it resembles a gargantuan combination lock, scattered over ten dimensions, that is missing its critical combination. All the same, we keep twisting and rotating the dials for an eternity, without every making any fundamental progress!

I have recognized, at least, that things are not always as they seem. That opportunism often masquerades as kindness, self-glorification as flattery, conceit as a virtue, raw profanity as cultivated civility, sublimated guilt as a play of innocence. It seems, far too shallow and barren a context to provide any real access to meaning. More like a dark tragicomedy and insufferable pantomime, in which all are wearing masks. The greatest costume party there has ever been! Nor can it bestow the love and attention, most deserve! Rarely, is there an ounce of genuine compassion expressed here at all. Most settle for those twisted, manipulative games of abuse, power, and control they call love.

Then there are times when I feel like a firework that has never left the ground. A spent force, close to being extinguished. Emotionally numb and increasingly immune to the insensitivities and vile actions of the world. There are days when I still feel some spontaneous compassion and laughter and others when I feel utterly exhausted of all goodwill for humanity. Sometimes, I suspect that the image and persona that walks and stalks the world bearing my name is an intruder. An inner gate-crasher, who has set me up to fail. Then as I adventure a little further down the rabbit hole, I come to suspect that maybe the world itself is the intruder and that I am merely a Patsy in my own life. Unquestionably, this world is living the high life by drinking from the cup of my vitality. Then it aims to poison all wells of my thought and spit me out like the dregs of yesteryear. Often, I ponder whether all the mental and physical toxins one accumulates from living here are what finally wipes one out.

Meanwhile, the shadow keeps following me about like a tyrannical master with a whip, reprimanding and objurgating me on my every move. Launching guilt trips for the most whimsical matters while prodding me with its stungun as a call to duty. It seems to be an alien force; I unwittingly invited in that has shanghaied the convoluted and nettled cosmos of my mind. One that constantly irritates and pesters the hell out of me, like a telemarketer that speed-dials at 3 am in the morning. Yes, I suspect there is something critically flawed at these worldly foundations that can never quite be repaired. Somehow, we can never put this Humpty Dumpty back together again."

(Jesus) Thanks for sharing this brief vignette of candid wisdom! If I were listening as a worldly psychiatrist, I would probably be sending you down the L-dopamine Hwy at this point and administering a regimen of ECT. Instead, I admire your raw and brutal honesty. It is good that the mantle of delusion and illusion that sits over your mind has been irreparably perforated. For you have found the crack in the psychic-matrix of the dreamworld and seen through its many deceptions.

Most here are numb, embittered and contracted to real life? Beneath their painted smiles, they conceal intense feelings of anxiety, frustration, animosity, and fear. Over time, their spontaneous outpourings become less and less. Some become hopelessly depressed and wonder where it all went wrong. Ponder why their thoughts are so bland and paper-mâché and why their insides feel like a rotting tomb. Eventually, their bodies begin to creak and groan like a famine ship, caught in a strong, stiff breeze in some old boatyard.

Then the death-wish kicks in. So their God of Death becomes their idol and Master. Through it, they hope to escape, at last, the burdensome misadventure of the Relative World—if only this were so! No, it will keep coming back to haunt because it has never existed on the outside. Instead, it is being continuously reborn and forged from within. Imaged in exact likeness to all their thoughts, desires, and fears. For this world can never be escaped through death, but only through Truth!

PROBING THE ILLUSORY NATURE OF THE RELATIVE

(Sharon) Where does the Relative World end and the Absolute begin?"

(Jesus) They never meet since they are mutually exclusive! The desire for the Relative causes the Absolute to completely disappear. You can only perceive the one you treasure. Choose illusion, and truth will lose all meaning. Nor can you truly appreciate truth, while you continue to welcome and uphold fugacious fantasies of the mind. The Relative World extends everywhere and encompasses everything you think and perceive. It is not just objects and phenomena that are insubstantial, but everything you reflect upon. All your sensations, perceptions, and conceptions are all equally untrue.

Hence, your thoughts are predominantly concerned with the non-existent and your obsessive reactions to a mere hallucination of the mind. You are ceaselessly being presented with a profoundly distorted picture fabricated out of your personal ego beliefs. Truth can never be recognized in the Relative Existence because all perceived there is entirely illusory. Instead, the highly potent and abstract becomes chopped into pieces, then sent through the blender so that it can be made to reflect your relative mind. Hence, it is shaped to fit that overly complex and ambiguous world formed from all your twisted wishes, toxic judgments, and fears. Thus must the limitless appear to be humbled and made to prostrate before your nonsense opinions. For how can truth ever provide irrefutable proof of its veracities within the dim distorting screen of the Relative?

(**Sharon**) Still, I was not convinced. Maybe this was all hocus-pocus nonsense J. was making up. I needed a more concrete and tangible explanation. So I asked, "**Can you explain to me the insubstantial nature of the Relative?**"

(**Jesus**) It is good that you are not easily swayed by mere words and ready to dive deeper. Jazzy rhetoric hypnotizes almost everyone in your world, and that is why lawyers, politicians, and entertainers do so well, while everyone else struggles. The first thing to fully realize is that everything in the Relative World has only a conditional reality. Each appearance arises from causes that are transient and unreal. When you probe the self-nature of every aspect, you find its dependence on a host of others and so on in an infinite regression. It is a labyrinth of relativities and interdependent causes in which all has become hopelessly tangled and intertwined. Nothing there has any intrinsic reality. Instead, each is as ephemeral as the marine layer or morning dew which evaporates quickly before the light of the sun. Like a soap bubble, it will pop in an instant, once its supporting context is melted through the power of reason.

Now let's start with some basics, by reviewing the world of sensation and perception. Doing so, we immediately grasp that all colors, sounds, tastes, smells and magnitudes only appear to exist through the contrast they make with others. Each is placed on a spectrum that is supposedly continuous. Apart from its position on this spectrum, it can provide no authentic witness, as to its existence. So does every aspect serve to reinforce the pseudo-reality of the others! When interrogated to provide proof of its reality, it merely points fingers towards its neighbors. The spectrum behaves then like a band of criminals, who quickly lie and collude to hide their individual parts in a cover-up.

For example, without silence as the essential backdrop, no sound could ever be heard. For, it would instantly lose its ability to emphasize its presence. Similarly, without sound, silence would go unrecognized. Notice also, how each sound depends intimately on its distinctive contrast to others to lend itself definition. Likewise, each color is entirely dependent on its variance for it to be perceived at all. If all were green, green would soon lose all meaning. Once you search for an Absolute green on the spectrum, you find it does not actually exist. Instead, you find there are a million different shades of green and beneath each of these, a million more and so on to infinity.

Similarly, it goes also with the perceptual worlds of taste, smell, magnitude, shape and form. Each aspect you probe has only a pseudo-reality and one that is contextually dependent. Apart from its surrounding context, none has any endogenous, self-substantiating reality of its own. In short, there can never be any mountain without a valley, nor any valley without a mountain; so it is with every aspect of the Relative Existence. It only seems to exist, because of the many games of comparison your mind continuously plays.

(Sharon) I had to admit; I detected a plausible elegance and logic in all this. It made me reminisce on an old Zen Koan, "*What is the sound of one-hand clapping?*" Now, for the first time, I understood its real meaning. Everything in the Relative World only appears to exist through its opposition to something else. No individual aspect has any clapping power of its own. All the boundaries and separations we establish are completely artificial. Then, once one realizes every object and phenomenon is merely an aggregate of illusory percepts and sensations, one immediately comprehends that nothing perceived in the Relative World genuinely exists at all. All, the same, I was on a roll and wanted to learn more. Consequently, I inquired, "**How does this extend to the world of concepts and symbols?**"

(**Jesus**) With the world of conceptual thought, we see the selfsame pattern emerge. Every concept depends intimately on its displacement to an opposing one. There can be no big without a small, no beautiful without an ugly, no sublime action without a dull and uncreative one. Everything awesome must have its so-so, and every virtue must have its vice. No beautiful woman has ever shown her face in public, without first insulting the uglier one. For it is she, after all, who makes the ugly woman seem all the more hideous.

Likewise, is masculinity defined by its departure from femininity and vice versa. Every statement simultaneously declares its inevitable war against an opposing one! Hence, a man who swears he is invincible is simultaneously claiming his lack of vulnerability. All that pretends to exist depends intimately on that which seems to exist not. Similarly, this world of relativity and context dependency holds true for symbols. No letter or word can stand on its individual merit because alone it retains no meaning. All letters need the collaboration and support of others. Words, in turn, are redundant in isolation. They must be formed first into sentences. All meaning in the relative existence is contextually derived. The Relative World is that special place, where everything seems to exist, but where nothing in fact does.

It is the Home of those blind to the Real. Those fumbling, groping creatures who use measuring tapes, spectrums, various conceptual vehicles, and contrivances in a futile quixotic attempt to hack their way back to the Real. Nevertheless, how can one measure the infinite or contain the limitless? On what particular spectrum can these ever be placed? How can one calibrate the potency, of that which is infinitely potent? Or establish ground level to that which fathomless? How do you stack-rank those who can barely spare a morsel of compassion, with the infinite Source of unconditional love and compassion?

In the Relative Existence, even the greatest of works will find their detractors, and an immense heap of dung, its admirers. The Relative World only arose out of the ego's specious, unsound judgments of what it alone considers worthy. Nonetheless, the ego's arbitrary assessments of what constitutes worth are without all merit. The ego possesses no Knowledge by which to appraise the immeasurable and immensely valuable. It can often hold great esteem for a big pile of dung while belittling the priceless and eternal in its midst! Then, seeing all its foolish ideologies reflected in this dung heap, it fast incorporates it into its hall of fame.

Thus, the Relative World becomes shaped and tainted from every angle by our severely opinionated minds. Meanwhile, the ego unceasingly vacillates. It makes endless backflips and compromises because it can know nothing for sure. Sooner or later, everyone is blackballed and painted with its dark brush. Whether they be a sinner or a saint, it makes no difference. They will be sent out to be tarred and feathered and humiliated in public. Because the ego born from the mud of erroneous beliefs, cannot tolerate seeing value in another.

(Sharon) I was beginning to glimpse the bigger picture. Grasping how judgment deprived us of Knowledge because it potentiates itself by emphasizing and apotheosizing differences. However, there can be no differences in that which is forever unified as One. Judgment, therefore, robbed us of vision. It was our unyielding stubbornness and closed- minded opinions that enabled the ego to flourish. This empowered it to unleash its full vehicle of deception. All of which strengthened the seeming validity of its senseless dictates.

Maintaining orders and hierarchies of illusion is only meaningful to those who would judge. Judgment, in turn, becomes idolized whenever we justify all illusory partitions, it arbitrarily establishes. Consequently, our many mindless endeavors to carve up Truth fashions this cruel ego self-portrait, known as the Relative Existence.

This all had me hooked. Reflexively, I asked, "**Is the Relative World simply a byproduct then of all our ego beliefs? A fantasy realm entirely architected out of our baseless judgments, and loss of Knowledge?**"

(Jesus) That's it, in a nutshell! Because of its inability to rightly evaluate and appraise, the ego has no choice but to amplify the unreal. Simultaneously it detracts from the eternally true. Projecting, its evil motives, everywhere, the shadow side soon becomes magnified out of all proportion. So the pure are tarnished, and the impure ennobled as gods. Thus, it can so easily justify tearing another apart. Yes every god will have its day in court, and each is to be crucified. In the end, the cumulative effect of all its corrosive thought patterns is to fashion the hellish landscape of your perception. All the ego's distortions and lopsided rationalizations shape and mold all that you perceive. Only, when you follow the guidance and inspiration of the Holy Spirit will all these distortions in your perception disappear.

(Sharon) It seems everyone is in on the scam and collaborates in perpetuating it. Those illusions of normalcy, decency, altruism, humanitarianism and togetherness are rampant everywhere one goes in bourgeoisie society. It can be all so sickening, nauseating and unspeakably repulsive at times. Each day I have to cross paths with the disgustingly self-righteous and all those ostentatious folk, who are so crafty at perpetrating stuffy airs about themselves. Their overbearing sense of righteousness and moral indignation has me clambering for the crapper faster than Usain Bolt. While I am in there, I start wondering whether now may be the right time to take a fistful of hollow-points and give them a few easy lessons in kinematics!

(Jesus) Yes, this world can only maintain its illusory deception through the twin poles of love and fear. Every thought, word or action is powered by these two primary visceral emotions. There is a spiritual tensor going on between good and evil, that provides the essential motive force for all its interplays and apparent motions. Only, in the relative existence, can God and the ego appear to be locking horns. All the same, Truth is not mocked by the ego, and this battlefield has never been real. It has merely become staged through your acceptance of falsities into your mind.

THE TINY MAD IDEA (TMI)

I was beginning to understand how all the psychodramas playing out in the world were the natural consequence of ego beliefs. Even so, something did not quite add up. So I put it out there! **"If Truth is so wonderful, then why did the relative existence ever come about?"**

(Jesus) This is the sanest and most reasonable question one could ever ask! However, those who believe fully in the Relative Existence will never ask it. Only those who have recognized its illusory nature must wonder how it came into pseudo-being. Then they immediately comprehend there must be another world beyond this one. After all, if we were perfectly content in Eternity, basking in pure bliss and glory, then why would we ever choose to enter hell? This question baffles the mind of all who seem bound to the Relative World. Likewise, if our Supreme Creator is all merciful and loving, why would He ever banish His Creations to a hopeless place? An insane depot, where they often actively wish for their deaths and destruction. You will soon learn the answers to these two vital psycho-spiritual concerns.

Firstly, you must realize that the strength of any masterful system of thought hinges on its capacity to answer the following three pivotal questions.

1. **Why did the Relative Existence come about?**

2. **How is it Maintained?**

3. **How can it be Relinquished?**

Just like the genie in the lamp, I am here to provide you with the answers to these three questions. You have no real trust in me as yet, but that will soon change. The answer to the first is a measure of the spiritual and metaphysical depth present in a particular system of thought. For it evidences how competently it traces to the initial cause. The answer to the second can be considered its breadth and scope. Because the explanation given must intelligently explain all the interactions, dynamics and cause-and-effect relationships present in the world of your perception as well as all the chaos, confusion, selfish motivations, and conflicting behaviors that serve to propagate it. Finally, the answer to the third question can be considered its height. For it is an indicator of the celestial heights to which it can rise. Can it reach to the stratosphere and provide the inspiration needed for following its teaching? Can it provide a clear-cut route out of the mess, that is guaranteed to work under all circumstances? You are the one who must evaluate if the proposed answer and resolution is meaningful and straightforward to follow. You must determine the consistency and lack of contradiction of what is being taught.

In the Relative World, you will find many different opinions on how it came about. Then there are those who think it has always been here. A scientist, for example, may declare it came into being with the Big Bang. An evolutionary biologist, in contrast, might contest that it derived from a single cell or strand of DNA. Some scientists believe in a Divine Creator, but conceive him as part of the fabric of the cosmos. Tightly interweaved, therefore into a universe, peripheral to themselves. Some evolutionary biologists see the divine as part of nature and its hub of intelligent and creative adaptations. Fundamentally these both misplace God because they attempt to fathom His essence in terms native to the Relative Existence. God, however, can have no part in fashioning the perceived world because of its chaotic, insane, impermanent and illusory nature.

As I said in "*A Course in Miracles*" the only cause of the relative existence was the **Tiny Mad Idea (TMI).** Once the Son contemplated this wild thought, he invited all illusions to infiltrate his mind. The can of ten-thousand worms had been opened, and all the hard work since has been merely to put the lid back on.

> **"Into eternity, where all is one, there crept a tiny, mad idea, at which the Son of God remembered not to laugh. In his forgetting did the thought become a serious idea, and possible of both accomplishment and real effects. Together, we can laugh them both away, and understand that time cannot intrude upon eternity. It is a joke to think that time can come to circumvent eternity, which *means* there is no time."**
>
> [ACIM, T-27.VIII.6:2-5]

Truth and Eternity remain ever-present and indestructible. It is a joke to think the eternal can disappear. It is just like a vast infinite sky, forever pervaded by the sunlight of unsurpassed wisdom. What is possible, is for dark clouds to block out the sun. This is exactly what happened, at that unholy instant, the Son mused on his TMI. Clouds soon hovered above which impeded the sunlight, and this gave rise to that bleak unreal world below, you now witness.

God could not prevent this from happening because He had always extended to his Son the free will to think and do as he wished.

The Son had it all and was on the spiritual equivalent of hookers and blow for all eternity. Then, in one ill-fated instant, he threw it all away. One foolish mishap and he quickly became barred from all the bliss and power of the Spiritual world. Most assuredly, the TMI was the fatal *faux pas* which unceremoniously ended the party. Sadly because the Son persists in taking the TMI and all its effects seriously, he continues to believe he is separate from his Eternal Home. Nonetheless, God never banished His Son from the Kingdom. It is the Son's tremendous guilt and sense of shame which alone excludes it from his awareness.

Once he realizes the TMI and all its effects remain unreal and laughs them off through forgiveness, he can restore back his elevated and visionary state of transcendental consciousness. Then the eternal will be self-evident, once more. Unfortunately, to this day, he continues to feel at the mercy of this dark world of his perception. In his fits of madness, he thinks he is outside the Kingdom. Blinded by all illusions, that plague his sight, he can no longer recognize his perfect Being, nor envision his exact likeness to his

Creator. Nevertheless, he still retains the power to Create and has never lost his divine inheritance.

(Sharon) This is all sounded very reasonable. My intuition spoke in very unambiguous terms, staunchly declaring that if the relative existence were ever real, then truth would be meaningless. Because a chaotic and meaningless place, impregnated with so much fear and evil, at every turn, could never be interwoven into a harmonious picture of Truth. Nor would its variable and unstable nature inspire any confidence. Likewise, I understood, that a God of unconditional love and mercy could ever banish his Son to hell, or even bear to be without him. Nor would unconditional love ever seek to take control or it would immediately become tainted. The element of subjugation would establish it had conditions and boundaries and therefore not be genuinely loving at all. It had to be the Son's choice to leave.

Thus God had indeed been a loving Creator and given free reign to His Son. Nonetheless, just as clouds are insubstantial vapor streams that can easily be shined away, the Son had the power to return the Kingdom to his awareness. All the same, what was the TMI? I was fascinated to learn more.

(Sharon) What exactly was the TMI?

(Jesus) The TMI was the Son's idle thought that he could usurp God's power by eating from the tree of knowledge. That fatal tree planted in the center of the Holy Garden was what induced Adam's sleep. It sullied his pure knowledge of the good by intermixing evil. The serpent convinced Eve that if they ate from it, they would no longer be dependent on God and hence could Create and thrive on their steam. This seductive thought, of being independent and yet equal to their Creator, drugged them with a dream of Specialness. Blinded and seduced by the allurement of this temptation forced them to give up the paradisiacal life. As I related in the Course:

> **"Eating of the fruit of the tree of knowledge is a symbolic expression for usurping the ability for self-creating. This is the only sense in which God and His creations are not co-creators. "**
>
> [ACIM, T-3.VII.4:1-2]

God had warned them never to eat from this tree for their personal wellbeing. Being the Source of unconditional Love and the Creator of Perfection, He alone knew all that worked. By corollary, any thought not present in His Mind would be retrogressive, harmful and guaranteed to fail. All such inefficacious thoughts, He designated '*evil*,' because they could never produce anything Creative. They merely represented delusions and idle fantasies of the mind. Ideas incapable of producing the eternally valid. Similar then to the various superpowers an imaginative kid may project to his toys when he invests them with peculiar capacities and abilities, they do not possess.

Unfortunately, Adam exercised his free will to go against God's advice. Prior to his tasting that fruit, he knew only of the Good. Regrettably, once the fruit was eaten, evil was known for the first time. This caused him to lose all access to Knowledge. Not that it was taken away, but it became shrouded. This was *the fall of Adam,* as spoken off in the Bible. It represents his foolish and failed attempt to gain power through the knowledge of evil.

> **"The fall of Adam and Eve is that they committed the sin of pride, believing that eating the fruit of the tree of the knowledge of good and evil would give them the wisdom of gods."**
>
> **[Bible, Genesis]**

All the same, evil cannot be known in any true sense be-cause it is not a Knowledge, but an anti-Knowledge. It,

therefore, functions, to veil Knowledge from one's awareness. By building a complex, convoluted maze of deception
around the mind it obscures the self-evident. The Course
Reference to the *'Tiny Mad Idea,'* has much in common
with *'The Fall'* of Adam, as spoken of in the Bible. It is that
moment when Adam fell into a deep sleep, from which he
has never awoken. To this day he remains asleep in the
Garden of Eternity. As I taught:

> **"Yet the Bible says that a deep sleep fell
> upon Adam, and nowhere is there
> reference to his waking up."**
>
> [ACIM, T-2.I.3:6]

This relative existence is Adam's dream world, and we are
Adam. It is a shabby and pathetic kingdom erected from
the fabric of illusions. One in which we seem to have lost
all power and control. Thus we walk about as petty trolls
within it, perpetually hounded by the insignificant and
blinded by our ego distortions. All of which keeps us fast
asleep until we voluntarily choose to awaken.

The Garden of Eden represents our pre-separation
Home—Eternity. The serpent represents Adam's free-will
and the unconscious wisdom of perfectly unified Being.

Namely, that transcendent Oneness beyond the scope of consciousness. in which no aspect is differentiated in any manner. Since the instant of the TMI, the Son has been wandering in a minefield of illusions, stepping on bouncing betties. He has never experienced a truly joyous belly laugh since. All his laughs are permeated with a certain cynicism and carry an unvanquishable despair. Only at the instant of Enlightenment, will he laugh again with a full-hearted, belly laugh!

WORLDLY ANALOGIES TO THE TMI

It seemed all too simple and convenient, yet I remained dissuaded. There was going to be no slick willy salesman putting one over on me. I decided to press on by fielding another question.

"You said earlier that the TMI invited illusions to enter the mind. Can you expound and clarify in more detail?"

(Jesus) The *Tiny-Mad-Idea*, was the first unreal thought to ever enter our minds. Since that unholy instant, nothing has been known with any clarity or confidence. For example, you are probably well aware of the cross-contamination phenomenon that is rampant everywhere in agriculture and industry. A minuscule trace of what is impure or toxic finds its way into another food source, and suddenly there is an industry wide recall or epidemic. Similarly, a small source of lead or another toxic chemical agent, once introduced to a pure water source can have devastating consequences, as seen recently in Flint Michigan.

In biology, entire ecosystems have been wiped out by the introduction of a new species or plant. This is because each ecosystem is a very sensitive and delicately tuned biodiversity system. It depends on numerous symbiotic and precisely timed interactions to survive. Once a foreign organism is introduced, the typical outcome is that entire breeds of animals, and other life forms start disappearing and wind-up on the endangered species list. Often new mutant forms of animal or plant life can develop that are dangerous, unsustainable or poisonous.

Similarly, thoughts do not exist in isolation. Each connects to a vast network of other ideas and concepts. Modifying even a single belief can have an immediate impact on the entire array of your beliefs. This effectively changes who you are, at least at the illusory level because it is from your process of thought that your identity emerges. Likewise, the TMI soon spread its contagion to other thoughts and beliefs, restructuring your belief system to one that fully endorses the imaginary. As a consequence, your world became darkened and swamped with illusions. All those dreams and fantasies you now cherish, or fear became projected from your erroneous beliefs.

This dissociative condition is known as **split-mind**, and it is one in which you cling tenaciously to false beliefs. Harboring the unreal becomes the fatal recipe that leads to contradictory patterns of thought. So your mind became distortionary, and you experience inevitable conflicts in your behavior. Thus you remain perpetually split and confused about yourself because when you endorse the unreal, you simultaneously cloud-out and deny the Real. The psychodynamics of projection and dissociation are what keep your illusion of split-mind intact. Thus you experience many symptoms tantamount to what has been called multiple-personality-disorder (**MPD**). Consequently, you witness a hallucinatory universe, which you yet take to be real.

Experiencing yourself as a split-mind does not change the eternal—only your awareness of the eternal. It cannot alter your original perfection, but it does cause you to lose sight of it. It is pure madness to conceive that Whole-Mind can ever be split or made discontinuous to itself. For example, when you peer through a kaleidoscope and rotate its front section you perceive a flood of different images. However, nothing real is being changed. All that is happening is a new reflection pattern is being produced, by your adjustment of the angle between two fixed mirrors. Similar is the case between Whole-Mind and your illusions of multiplicity. You witness millions of different bodies and minds that seem apart only because your unsound beliefs create distortion, which is like adjusting the angle.

Imagine Truth as one of these mirrors and your mind as the other. When your mind is 100% harmonious with Truth, both mirrors are in perfect alignment, and consequently, no pattern emerges. Hence, you just perceive a transparent light-filled image with no distortions. Now consider all your incorrect beliefs, as functioning to adjust the angle between these two mirrors. The distortion of the adjustment angle produces all the bodies and false perceptions you see in the world around you. However, they are not genuinely separate from you, anymore than you are from Truth. They remain part of your Whole-Mind. As you rotate the mirror of your mind back into alignment with Truth, you will once again recognize unity as all pervasive. Then all false patterns, bodies, and images disappear from your perception.

We can never lose our Divine Inheritance because what God gives is Eternal. Our Mind remains forever radiant and immaculate. Our original perfection and abundance can never be compromised, but we can get that impression, while we seem to inhabit the distortionary landscape of illusion. Whenever you are diverting the adjustment angle of our consciousness away from Truth, by retaining incorrect beliefs, many exotic and fearful images will appear in your dream landscape.

(Sharon) If God is so unconditionally Loving, Why would He place a Tree that could lead to our downfall in the very center of the Garden?

(Jesus) The center of the Garden is merely symbolic. It means the tree was positioned at the root Source of all for our protection. His Mind was the Holy Fountain from which emanated unconditional Love, light, and the power behind all Creation. Being the Prime Creator of Perfection, He alone possessed the Knowledge of what was Creative. Any foreign and superfluous quantity, unknown to Him, would, therefore, be uncreative, redundant and detrimental. He knew all such pointless thoughts were dangerous and distractive and therefore to be avoided at all costs. They became collectively known by what is termed evil. However, being loving He could deny his children no part of their freedom. He maintained an open-doors policy at all times and had no room barred or with restricted access. All the same, being naughty and mischievous children, we decided to use our free will to barge through this door, and nothing has been the same since.

(Sharon) If the TMI was an entirely unreal idea, it must have been innocuous! How then could it cause so much devastation?

(Jesus) Firstly, as an idea, it remains innocuous because all the devastation you now perceive is only at the level of illusion. Secondly, it does not take too much imagination to understand how a single thought or action can lead to extreme affliction downstream. Even at the mundane level, we often see how a single virus can bring down an entire organism or even result in a pandemic. Destructive power is not about quantity but relates instead to inbuilt potential. A single idea can quickly proliferate to unleash a veritable contagion of mind-poisons.

All forms of genocide, for example, are built on a single root idea—the supposed inferiority of some race, class, religion or sect. Over the last hundred years alone, this single misplaced idea has led to the brutal murder of millions, as well as countless other atrocities. Ideas spread like wildfire once a mind finds them attractive. A glitzy cover or sweet taste are often all that is needed for it to go viral. Unattractive ideas, in contrast, are denied and repressed and soon rendered unconscious. They do their nasty work in the underground leading to all manner of neuroses and psychoses.

Many ideas, hateful dogmas, and delusive worldly systems are nothing but chocolate covered poisons. You are sold hell, but first, receive a slice of heaven. This is how the cocaine, crystal meth, and opioid epidemics have flourished in recent times. It is how all pernicious and evil ideologies grow. Genocide is just one example. We likewise see how the power of marketing lies in its capacity to sell an underlying falsity under the veneer of some quaint tale or aphorism. You become hooked initially on what you found mildly appealing. But soon it becomes psychologically compelling. You may, for example, be sold on a dream of your exclusivity through purchasing a certain extravagant but unneeded product or by a particular image that costs. The ego is very cognizant of all these tactics and is always up to mischief to empower itself.

Other examples include bridges, superstructures, and viral videos. With superstructures, the devastation that tears them apart is often triggered by a tiny vibration or stimulus. All of which leads to an under-damped resonance that is sustained through positive feedback. The original stimulus becomes amplified to the point that the bridge or superstructure can no longer contain it. In the case of a dam or weir, a single piece may fracture or displace to let a tiny rivulet of water pass through at its weakest point. The positive feedback of force created by this small stream causes an even larger fracture to develop. Soon, a greater flow of water passes through this fracture location. Within moments the result can be catastrophic, and the whole dam collapses.

You may have wondered why a particular video takes off, while a thousand similar videos remain stillborn? Usually, the viral explosion is caused by something as trivial, as the initiator deciding to pass it on to one additional person. Suppose these two recipients, between them, choose to relay it forward to three others or more. Then the critical forwarding momentum needed to support sustained positive feed-forward is established since the number passing it forward exceeds the number not bothering to do anything at all. Consequently, the video soon goes viral. It is very much like a pyramid scheme in the communication world. Often the mass hysteria produced mystifies the initiator because the final response seems amplified out of all conceivable proportions.

Other examples of these dynamics are found everywhere. They include lasers, chain reactions, exponential growth in bacteria colonies, pandemics, etc. With lasers, the final high energy beam is often created from a single photon. The triggering photon is forced to displace at least one other before being reflected. This sustains positive feedback between the two reflecting mirrors, and the original photon becomes amplified into a light beam of high intensity.

In a similar manner, the darkness inherent in the TMI soon spread like an unavoidable and unruly contagion. The positive feedback of guilt reinforced the original source of darkness. Once we declared one person as guilty, it became easier to see everyone as guilty. Once we deemed another as separate, we appeared to enter a world of separation. Perhaps you are familiar with holistic theory and with Indra's net. In Holistic theory, what affects the part will also affect the whole and vice versa. This is because the part is just a microcosm of the whole. So it is with the TMI. It soon contaminated the entire world of our thoughts and beliefs.

Indra's net is a cascade of jewels in which the image in each is reflected in all the others. Thus the individual splendor of each jewel is seen all the more radiant. However, once we place a dark patch on any one of the gems, this spot shows up also in the others. This inhibits their collective reflecting power. Consequently, the entire array soon becomes dark and lusterless.

The TMI was the all-important launch-pad that set the relative world in motion. It represents that pivotal event which signaled our fall from divine awareness. It became catastrophic to how we experienced ourselves. Afterward, we had no choice but to interpret our identity through the distorting prism of this dark world with its perpetual haze of a gazillion nasty reflections. There was nothing left to guide us because we were no longer in tune with Knowledge. A loss that caused us to go insane. All the same, the monumental effects of the TMI often seem astounding when compared to their original cause.

"No one asleep and dreaming in the world remembers his attack upon himself. No one really believes there really was a time when he knew nothing of a body, and could never have conceived this world as real. He would have seen at once that these ideas are one illusion, too ridiculous for anything but to laughed away. How serious they now appear to be! And no one can remember when they would have met with laughter and with disbelief. We can remember this, if we but look directly at their cause. and we will see the grounds for laughter, not a cause for fear."

[ACIM, T-27.VIII.5:4-10]

Just as a collapsed dam can flood numerous towns and villages and even wipe out livelihoods nowhere near the impact zone, so it is with the TMI. It displaced the unassailable Peace and perfect Knowledge resident in the Mind of the Son from all conscious awareness.

(Sharon) You said before that the psychodynamics of projection and dissociation keep our illusion of split-mind in place. Can you explain this and how they are related to the TMI?

(Jesus) The TMI represented our failed attack on the sovereignty of God. It was the belief we could usurp our Heavenly Creator and steal His Power for ourselves. This ungrateful and calculating thought has driven us mad with guilt. Even though our guilt was misplaced and could never have any real effects, we could not live with ourselves because of it, nor could we die. Nor could we bear to be in God's Presence because of our profound sense of guilt and shame.

The only other possibility was to fool our own minds into thinking a part of us was pure, innocent and perfect while the rest was laden with guilt. This produced the dissociation known as split-mind in which Whole-Mind seems to become fragmented into many. In our attempt to alleviate the pain of our guilt, we became positively schizophrenic. Our Whole-Mind appeared to dissociate into millions of separate bodies and minds. Each mind now seems to be housed separately in its own special piece of clay and buys in completely to the ill-founded belief that it can operate independently. This insane condition is an essential feature of the relative existence. It is one in which each aspect seems self-banished into a private kingdom and is unrelated to the rest. This private kingdom serves also to protect it from the vengeance it fully expects from God. Each is a world of multiplicity and form—one of many useless objects and phenomena.

In our sickened mindsets, we continue to believe we have impeached God and robbed Him of His power. This power we project instead to various external agents. We project it to Nature and Science and the duplicitous gods of our ego selves. We conceive that it is Nature that sustains and supports our being. Thus have we created numerous false idols as our proxies for Reality. The faceless gods of Science, Biology, Genetics, Technology and Economics, have risen fast to become top dogs in our universe. We see these as the causal powers that drive and perpetuate our existence. Ones who establish our immortal signatures and genetic footprints. Ones who determine our entire life-range, scope, predispositions, and potentialities. Overnight they have arisen to become veritable Molochs that we prostrate deferentially before. Our many sacrifices to them, include our lifeblood, faith, and industry. Even so, they constitute nothing more than mind-produced surrogates standing in for the divine. Self-made gods, through whom we hope to dethrone our Creator.

Nonetheless, the TMI never had any real effects, and none of this ever happened. All maddening effects and bleak appearances we perceive will only remain in view as long as we believe our fall from God genuinely occurred. Any moment we can heal ourselves by purging all our misplaced guilt, through forgiveness. So are our minds restored to full awareness of the Kingdom!

THE PSYCHO-GENESIS OF OUR DENIAL

(Sharon) J. had certainly made it seem feasible how a single wrong idea can take hold to wreak supreme devastation. After all, we see it all the time in the stock market. An unsubstantiated rumor can suddenly trigger a panic or sell-off. Similarly, wars are often triggered by a single minor incident and often lead to tens of millions of deaths downstream. Likewise, every so often we see various fads take off, for no apparent reason. Everything from cabbage patch dolls to hula hoops to large transistor radios, flatscreen TVs, and i-Phones. One has to wonder if these hyped-up trends are designed to fill some giant gaping hole in ourselves. Whether they are simply ego maneuvers that temporarily prevent us from going outright mad. Compensations designed to shield our awareness from the essential meaninglessness of our lives?

Nevertheless, usually, a simple mistake can be easily rectified if addressed upfront. Doing so can often undo or alleviate all the damage. Why hadn't Adam and Eve just laughed it all off, as J. had said? Realized their scheme was not working and immediately atoned for their mistake? So I put this question forward to J.

(Jesus) Sometimes it is as simple as that, and sometimes it isn't. Like you said, if only they addressed it immediately, but they didn't. Adam and Eve thought for certain that they could rule in their own special kingdom. They didn't want to admit to failure and come back to God with their tails dragging between their legs. As a result, they soon were caught in a very convoluted web of denial. Then after entering the deep sleep of ignorance, they could no longer think sanely. Soon all sorts of crap started to hit the fan which rapidly made their situation all the more irredeemable. You need to understand the full mechanics of denial.

Firstly there is usually a triggering cause. Usually this is some seed desire, thought or event that fast establishes an untenable situation. The primary symptom of which is so repulsive and unbridgeable that it must be consciously denied. Soon various perpetuating forces or agents creep in that keep the roots of what is denied from ever being looked at again. Finally, some vicious cycle is established that places the source of what is rejected entirely out of one's conscious awareness.

```
TRIGGERING CAUSE
(SOME DESIRE, EVENT OR IDEA)

PRIMARY SYMPTOM

PERPETUATING FORCES

VICIOUS  CYCLE
```

DENIAL

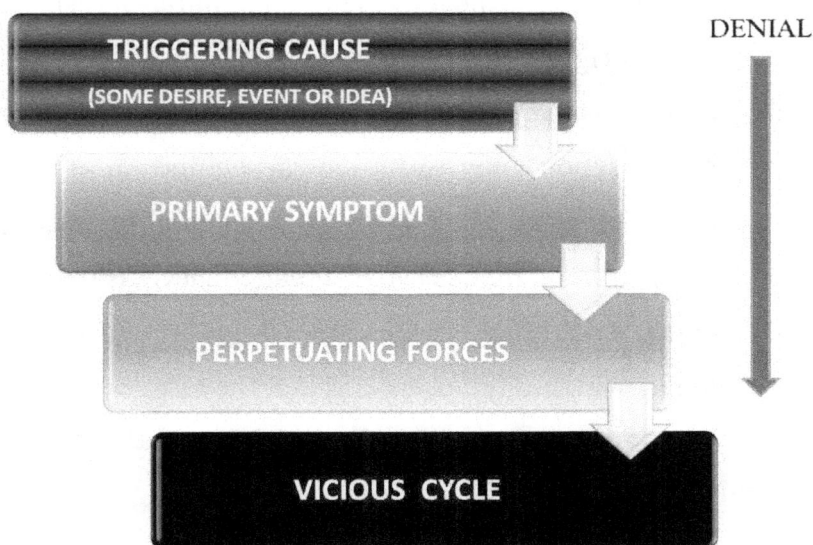

THE CAUSE-AND-EFFECT PROPAGATION OF DENIAL

(Sharon) This all sounds elegant, but I need some strong, elucidating examples to understand the nuts and bolts of it all.

(Jesus) Take abuse for example. The triggering event is the abusive act itself. The primary symptom is often a deep feeling of unworthiness and shame. The perpetuating force is often the strange notion that one is personally responsible for what happened. This, unfortunately, is the case for most victims of abuse, molestation, incest, rape, etc. Their feelings of personal culpability and shame often become a blocking agent to all healing. This poor initial interpretation of the original event often causes them to go rapidly downhill. Thus they close up shop and withdraw from all future interaction, only to hide away behind an array of self-made defenses. Their feelings of culpability often go on to perpetuate a vicious cycle of inadequacy, disgust, and self-attack. It can degenerate into a total lack of trust in everyone, including themselves. Then they can become alienated and increasingly self-destructive, and the final result is often tragic.

(Sharon) How does all this relate to the TMI?

(Jesus) With the TMI, the primary cause was our desire for specialness. We wanted to be able to Create apart from God and be entirely independent of Him. When we realized this would never work, the primary symptom we experienced was guilt and also a great sense of shame. After all, He had freely given us the Kingdom of Bliss and shared all His Love and Power with us. We, as the Son of God had been placed in a very elevated position. One even higher than that of the angels. We felt our own betrayal of his faith and trust in us, to be ten thousand times greater then than that of Judas. Just as Judas had gone off to hang himself, we chose to hide away in this private illusory kingdom of our own making. We came to hate ourselves for the ingratitude we had demonstrated. We could no longer tolerate being in His Presence. The unconditional love He freely bestowed, now seemed unmerited, even suffocating. Eventually, our guilt became mostly unconscious, but its effects remain to this day. Its effects are the relative world each of us perceives. One that reflects our own guilt and self-hatred everywhere we go.

In this Relative Existence, each finds themselves in a very problematic position. It is only natural that each seeks to project the cause of this sad state of affairs, to various causes "outside" their mind. Moreover, once your mind becomes unloving, it possesses no real clarity anymore. It falls into a deep state of sleep, dreaming dark dreams of fear, guilt, evil and sin. It nurses all manner of idle fantasies in which it is sole ruler in its own unique and special kingdom. In its madness, it thinks it can create in the absence of God. I have referred to this in the Course as '*The Authority Problem.*' Along with ever-present guilt and our deep state of sleep, it functions to perpetuate the relative existence. Since each projects their guilt to "others," a vicious cycle of Separation, Fear, Judgment and Defense is established. One that keeps each trapped in the relative existence and unwilling to probe further the real source of their guilt.

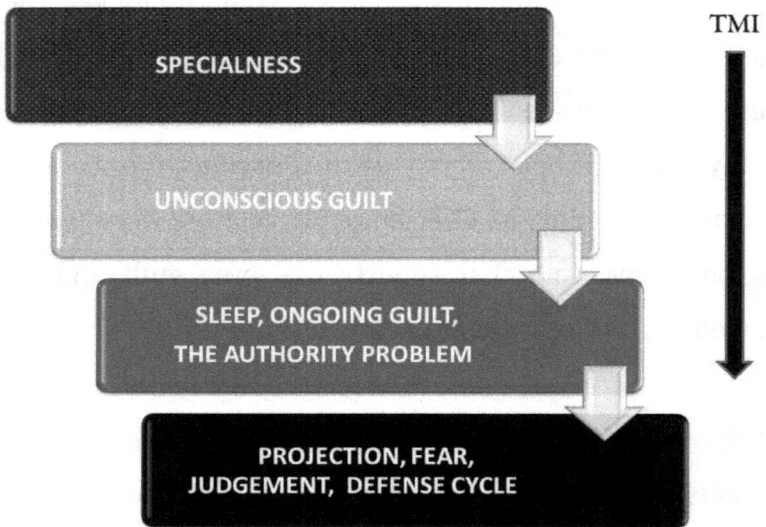

THE CAUSE-AND-EFFECT PROPAGATION OF THE TMI

Yes, denial is rampant in the Relative World. Everyone goes about dressing up the mannequin in flashy clothes and jewels — trying to make it look beautiful for as long as they can. Unfortunately, most are unwilling to peer just below the surface. That is why you see so many ingenious euphemisms abounding in the Relative World. There is a great fear of naming things for what they are. There is no doubt that life can feel groovy at times. Times when we can feel no end to all the magic, mystery, and surprise. Simply look at all those crazy new inventions designed to continuously bombard our senses with sensual pleasure waves of absolute ecstasy. Often one may be held in awe, just marveling at it all. All those opportunities that simply dazzle and impress. All those trustworthy friends, whose light continuously inspires. Maybe you are already looking forward to a well-deserved retirement. Already in the planning phase of your cruises and world travels. In these, you hope to fulfill at last a number of lifelong ambitions. At the very least you expect to catch some soul-soothing rest.

Maybe you don't buy-in completely to all those dreams of success sold to you by the flees in the marketplace? Perhaps the depth of your self-delusion is already beginning to show its fruit, and you are glimpsing how opportunities don't always track your potential to a tee. Perhaps you have not reaped the rewards you expected from a lifetime of wise investments. Reflecting on it a little more, you get a whiff of some dark invisible conspiracy — something deeply codified operating just below the threshold of your conscious awareness.

Somehow the right opportunities have always gone astray, and your music remains unsung. Like the dodo bird, you were always deprived of the right wings to fly and now are heading fast towards obsolescence. Feeling one final onslaught of humiliation as the profiteering enterprises take their last stab at your dignity while friends of a lifetime slowly drift away. Perhaps you have already begun to feel like some dissipated and dilapidated carcass in a purgatory, just waiting for the bodily bonfire to burn itself to cinders?

There are some, whose lives become ornamented fast by a bleak catalog of tragedies, suicides, and untimely deaths. Of too many steam-trains, coming from nowhere, targeting the epicenter of their efforts. So now they feel profoundly disenchanted, emotionally numbed-out and thoroughly lobotomized by their senseless existence. Finally beginning to glimpse the full insanity of it all in full 4k UHD. Often in some epiphanic moment, the true harvest of their denial becomes abundantly clear. Then they lucidly capture all the world's brutalities and despairs, all its wasted endeavors and meretricious enticements. It is certainly a Kodak moment. One that entices them to listen and voyage deeper to the real cause of it all. For they are no longer hypnotized by its twisted deceptions and flimsy temptations.

But most do not want to peer beneath the painted veil of the world. Expecting, it will be far too painful. So they remain caught in their web of denial and seek salvation only at the surface.

(Sharon) You are preaching to the converted. This world just keeps getting shallower by the day. The robots are everywhere now. It seems the well of authentic humanity is rapidly running dry. Replaced by a nexus of zombies who spend all their time texting elevator conversations to each other — living and dying by their cyber-profile likes. Most do not tap anywhere near their full potential. Their lives remain unwritten slates of pure potentiality, never harnessed. Others could be considered super-candidates for the Darwin award.

I find most are afraid of death, but even more afraid of living. Many cannot tolerate any real risk, slight or loss of face and dread being made to square off with their personal demons. The majority of humanity are their own worst enemy and yet do not realize it because the degree of their denial is too great! We are forever self-sabotaging our lives with the inner poisons of our fear, shyness, laziness, inertia and low confidence. So we hide away in the modern day caves of our apartments and cubicles while ceaselessly trolling online. We are always pretending to be someone glorious, special and adventurous that we most certainly are not.

Nor does this ego world provide the ideal environment for unleashing our full potential. The tremendous gifts of sensitive souls are too often ignored, put down, or ridiculed in the most brutal and merciless ways. Most corporations seek to institutionalize us into being mere cyborgs of their One-Mind Nexus 6 work cultures. They will employ any tactic that denies our tremendous creativity and worth. Nor to they want us to recognize our freedom. The assembly of perks is there to steal away our lives little by little. A content masked by an array of tawdry enticements. So the eternal Son of God roams about the farm as a mere minion. Accepting his lot, as an organic android who needs to placate the bloodthirsty gods of big industry. He bends over for the whip and graciously accepts a host of outrageous demands, insurmountable task-lists and a flurry of unrealistic expectations.

Our innate abilities are not the problem — rather it is the continuous erosion of our self-belief and self-esteem, that can break our spirit. Not to mention all the crap hiding out in our psychological knapsacks. The first skeleton I pull out, are all those "friends" who constantly badger and coerce us and incessantly leech from us. Always there to take us for what we have while functioning as enemies and anti-catalysts to our dream progress. It is easy to see why many resort to the ego's bag of conjuring tricks and quick patches to create some semblance of a life.

Is it a genuine wonder then that the circus of our lives contains so much anarchy, turbulence, and commotion? Considering there are always far more clowns than spectators? Is it a surprise that our psyches mirror the Grand Canyon, having become deeply lacerated by the multi-billion year ice-ages of the soul? Are we shocked to find all former peaks in our self-confidence have been erased from all the villainous assaults, we have endured, from every fiend and succubus that roams our underworld? Each seeking to eviscerate from the fear-frozen nugget of our hearts any residual trace of our former integrity and self-respect. Yes, this ego world aims to break us down at every turn. It wants to have us crawl about and grovel like beaten dogs so that we willingly prostrate before its pillars of dust.

(Jesus) It may surprise you to hear, that you did not always experience your existence this way. Yes, once timelessness alone was known and entertaining this Relative World of spacetime, bodies, and a gazillion trivial things would have been considered the height of madness. Instead, you lived cradled in the arms of Love and even your most idle thought was golden. For each of your thoughts held unimaginable power and was capable of immersing itself completely in the full matrix of life and potentiality. From here, peace spread-out in never-ending circles of joy, enlivening and intoxicating all with its heavenly perfume of pure ecstasy. Every moment new and fragrant worlds would parade before your grand vision, bringing to you, light, truth and meaning.

In this glorious realm, there was no sickness, death or destruction. No torrents of vengeance, hatred, and despair, nor any other banners to lifelessness. No whirlpools of insanity that could overrun the mind, nor any pestilential forces set to derail your efforts. Instead, all was immaculate and indestructible. Oh, how things have changed, since that fatal moment when the Son remembered not to laugh.

(Sharon) You have got me motivated now! I would like to get more detail on our '*Authority Problem*'! Because it still seems to me that God was running some Loving Dictatorship. One in which he always held the Trump card, and we were absolutely justified and wise in getting the hell out of there.

THE SON'S ABSOLUTE DEPENDENCE
ON GOD

(Jesus) If God were running a dictatorship, he would never have given us free-will. Unconditional love always seeks to set free because it knows a relationship based on control and manipulation is not truly loving at all — only toxic and contractive. One of the hardest actions a parent ever has to make is to let their children go. It can tear them apart inside when they see their children making alarming mistakes or even becoming overtly self-destructive. But a loving parent is there simply to provide help, never to take-over.

Our '*Authority Problem*' succinctly put, is our strange belief that we can create ourselves. However, this belief is pure nonsense, when examined up close. It would be like a light ray declaring itself to be both the bulb and source of its individual light. Similarly, when we seek to stand above God in the greater scheme of things, we are asking for the impossible and ignoring the inescapable fact that God must always be above us. Not that He is above us qualitatively, but only because of His crown position in the causal relationship. God will always remain, **The Creator of Perfection**, while we the Son will always remain, **A Creator of**

Perfection. We are powerless without God, but God also needs our loving help to extend His Masterful Work of Creation. The light of Creation we bring has the same quality as that of our Source. However, even though we are made of light we are not the Creators of the light we shine.

It is this desire for Self-Authorship that led to the apparent fall from grace. It did not change *who we Are, only our awareness of who we Are*. Our specialness desire caused us to lose sight of our original Perfection. Our stubborn, childish belief that an effect can be its own cause keeps us relegated to that illusory kingdom, known as the Relative Existence. There we go stomping about like Don Quixotes chasing after shadows and tilting at the many windmills of life. Declaring ourselves emperors while in reality we are wearing rags and falling apart. This world of separation is nothing more than a game of denial, in which we refuse to acknowledge both the incontrovertible logic and irreversibility of Truth. It is nothing but a game of make-belief that should be quickly laughed off.

(Sharon) Why can't an effect be its own cause?

(Jesus) Only a severely deluded mind could ever ask such a question! You have been hanging around in the Relative World for far too long, where such nonsense questions can often seem meaningful and even sane. Then again, folk in that madhouse are continuously reversing true cause-and-effect relationships. Often also they attribute causes to the non-existent. Let me riddle you this! Can a Son be his own Father? Can a bodily disease be real, when the body itself is an illusion? Can a software program develop itself?

(Sharon) But intelligent software learning algorithms do exist in which software programs can enhance and heuristically optimize themselves.

(Jesus) The software is merely re-parameterizing itself based on outcomes. All the decision algorithms and constraints for those redevelopments and optimizations are established by the programmer and his or her code. The source code itself is not being overridden by the program. When you look closely, you will see that no effect can ever be its own cause.

(Sharon) How about an electrical control loop? Every part of the control circuit is both a cause and effect and critical to the smooth operation of the other parts. Similarly, we see this in the circulatory system of the body. The heart pumps the blood that keeps the brain alive and yet the brain controls the pumping action and rhythm for the heart! Similarly, all ecosystems survive and flourish through the development of symbiotic and co-dependent relationships. Each organism seems to be instrumental in driving all the improvements and adaptations seen in its neighbors.

(Jesus) Whenever you see cause-and-effect circularity, you can be sure that the actual cause is outside that system. With a control loop, the real cause is in the Engineer's mind who puts all the intelligent pieces together. Similarly, with the circulatory system of the body, the real Cause is the intelligent awareness behind it all. This awareness you cannot see, because it is not any thing. Yet it is this awareness that projects the body and assigns it all its functions. For the same reason, no real cause will ever be found in the Relative Existence, but only from outside this manifold.

An ecosystem is just like the human body. All the elements work together to achieve a common purpose. All the same, one can immediately comprehend that it would be foolish to say a leg is the cause of an arm or an arm that of a leg. The real cause once again is outside the body and within the mind that projects the body. Even in an ecosystem, the cause is also very much outside it. It is in the weather patterns and the natural environment which then provide the supporting context for it to flourish. Freeze you tropical ecosystem to 30 below zero and see how long it survives.

(Sharon) What would happen if an Effect could be its own Cause?

(Jesus) A most excellent and progressive question for a change. Apart from the fact that it is impossible, the results would be disastrous. If everything could be its own cause, all notions of there being any real cause or effect would instantaneously cease. With no dependency, there would be no gel to keep all the elements together. The result would be increased isolation and exclusion and many other catastrophic consequences. Since each element would be independent, the system would soon disperse or collapse.

Similarly, if we were independent of our Creator, then our creations would also be independent of us. Being independent, they would be able to disappear from sight or even destroy themselves. We would be powerless to prevent this. As a result, we would soon find ourselves in a joyless isolated kingdom all on our own. Our personal creations would therefore relegate our role as their Creator null and void.

Each could easily construct an impermeable bubble around itself and seal itself off from its creator. Thus our creative power would be limited exclusively to our individual efforts. We would, therefore, be unable to leverage our shared creative power in order to create something truly awesome. Realistically, alone we have no creative power. Even in the Relative Existence, this is evident. It takes many minds working creatively on a problem to make all the wizardry you now see. All the neat evolutions in technology, medicine, automation, food science, rocket-ry, etc. could never happen if so many did not come to-gether to achieve a common goal. Left alone, we would still be driving Flint mobiles and filing our tax returns with the help of an abacus.

When nothing is shared, all the magic and joy soon evapo-rates. It would be akin to taking a vacation or cruise on one's own. In the end an empty experience and incompa-rable to going with a host of friends. Perhaps you are aware that prisoners stuck in solitary confinement for long periods often hallucinate images or else project their thoughts to inanimate objects. All so that, they can share something with someone, even if it is just an hallucination. Yes! Nothing is real unless it can be shared. Many in the Relative World have gone mad from isolation. Many others have become pretty lifeless and sick because they are afraid of others and their environment. So they hide away behind a barrage of defenses. What they fail to realize, is these "others" that they fear, are colored by the projection of their own fear-based thoughts.

So this chain of dependency between Creator and creation is a good thing. It empowers us to leverage our collective efforts. We should be grateful to our Creator for protecting our best interests. *'The Authority Problem'* is the inbuilt safety mechanism that guarantees the Kingdom will never self-destruct, discombobulate or come apart. Instead, it will always grow and increase in its creative power. As creations, we are all codependent and share the same Mind.

(Sharon) How does it all work?

(Jesus) Since you are familiar with multi-CPU parallel pro-cessing systems and architectures, you know that they can extensively increase their efficiency by leveraging a shared memory pool. Each processor puts the results of what it has learned into this pool so that other processors can use it. Thus each gains by taking advantage of the completed tasks of others. Since they all work together synergistically in the path of their shared interests, their collective effi-ciency and processing power is increased.

Likewise, God sought to both protect and enhance the Kingdom. So he put an important measure into the Creative process. He decided we would all share a single Mind, through which we would all be able to communicate perfectly with each other. Thus we could each freely share our creative work with every aspect of mind. It is like Open-Source code of the spiritual variety. Creation works through authenticating and assimilating the thoughts of our shared Mind. Only when all aspects are in full agreement on what is lovable and good, can it be extended. Only then is it Real. So it is not a democracy or a rule by numbers game in which the opinion of the majority or ruling elite gets to trounce that of minorities.

Nor is it a plutocracy, oligarchy or dictatorship, but a form of rule through complete inclusion and total agreement. More like a pure, benevolent democracy, in which every mind can pull the plug if it does not like what is sees. One in which all serve as guardians over the unprotected thoughts of others. Once any single aspect disagrees on the merit of what is created through thought, that thought never makes it onto the red carpet. It never becomes part of Creation. This system is good, because if one son builds a big pile of dog manure, another should not be expected to appreciate it for all eternity.

(Sharon) It seems a very Utopian system and one in which nothing would ever get done. Instead, we would all sit around like a bunch of old ladies hemming and hawing forever. No wonder I can find no word for it in the Relative Existence.

(Jesus) Yes, in the Relative Existence this system would never work. So many interfering egos poisoned by their personal agendas to bother to see through the eyes of another. That is why there are so many executive orders, wars and communication breakdowns. In fact, if everyone in the Relative Existence could agree on a single thing, the dream of the Relative Existence would disappear. This is because anything shared unambiguously across all of Mind automatically produces the Real. Remember, the Relative Existence only came about because the Son tried to go against God. All the same, because this thought was unshared, all effects streaming from it remain unreal. The Son, therefore, can only produce a world of illusions. One in which he continues to think unreal thoughts.

It is like he has his wings clipped, whenever he attempts to get up to any mischief on his own. This seems somewhat like a dictatorship, in which God is saying "*It is My way or the Highway,*" but there are good reasons behind it. God is after all a loving parent. Whenever he sees his Son around fireworks or explosives, the matches are taken away and the Son's creative power is rendered entirely innocuous. This is God's means of guaranteeing the Son will never harm himself. The Son can fantasize that he has set off the explosives, but that is all.

However, the Son was not happy with the arrangement despite all its necessary fail-safes. He sought the specialness of being *'The Sole Creator of Perfection.'* Thus he continues to hide about sulking until he gets his way, which is the real meaning of the parable of the Prodigal Son. Like the Prodigal Son, he thinks he can do better on his own. In his dreams, he imagines that he has accomplished his kingdom. It remains an illusory kingdom built on nothing but his drug of specialness. So he feels powerless and thinks he is outside the gates. He has become a tattered reflection in the mirror feeding off the dregs and sad offerings of the Relative World. A pathetic Orwellian figure who finds himself down-and-out everywhere he goes.

Nevertheless, he continues to prance about like some Mafioso Godfather and to believe himself a self-made man. He remains in obvious denial of the fact that he has no real wealth here and is merely traipsing about in a broken down body eating the slops, given to the pigs. When he denied his Creator, he also denied the Source of his real Creative Power. Even so, God never denied him anything and still holds open the gates to the Kingdom. He has given us the keys, yet we are too ashamed to go Home. So does each dream image mistakenly think it is self-sustaining! It romanticizes that it can architect for itself success without any cooperation from its Source. However, all it can architect is a terrifying dream. The *'Authority Problem'* meanwhile remains the root of all appearances of evil.

> **"I have spoken of different symptoms, and at that level there is almost endless variation. There is, however, only one cause for all of them: the authority problem. This is "the root of all evil."**
>
> [ACIM, T-3.VI.7:1-3]

The Son's *'Authority Problem'* is the real reason that you see so many egos flying about thinking they are masters of the universe. Their own comfort and well-being are their primary concerns. They devote all their energy expenditures and thought propaganda towards protecting their bodies, reputations, and interests. 99.9% of what they do is for themselves. They have the fight or flight mentality and are continuously seeking to enlarge their life-spaces. No number of heads strung up and hanging over the kitchen table is enough. So some, proudly string them around their necks and wear them like a mala of mantra beads. Then they go about chanting in harsh dissonant tones, their ego mantras dedicated to the gods of specialness. The desire for specialness is one of the primary causes of all the evil showing up in the world. It is the motive that fuels so many acts of thoughtlessness, brutality, and mercilessness. Like all insubstantial dream idols, the damage caused can be greatly exacerbated through projection.

> **"When you have the authority problem, it is always because you believe you are the author of yourself and project your delusion onto others."**
>
> [ACIM, T-3.VI.8:2]

Due to projection of our 'Authority Problem', we think others are against us, rather than part of us. After all, if we can self-create and be our own man-gods, why cannot they? Thus we see each as an independent being who can successfully attack and steal from us. The result is all-out ego wars with parts of our greater Self. We do not project our power solely to "others," but to everything we see in the Relative World. So we project the source of our physical sustenance to the gods of nature, nutrition, and medicine, and aim to obviate God entirely in the equation of our existence.

Projection of power away from our inward Source is the reason so many worldly belief systems thrive. By projecting our power to the screen of the world, we have enabled the modern false gods of science, genetics, materialism, economics etc. to become empowered. Since not everyone is ready to accept such modern villains as their gods, we also see a rise in atheism and agnosticism. Likewise, we project various powers to our dream images. We think our ingenuity, imagination, misplaced efforts and ruthlessness can get us what we want. Then when things are not working out as hoped, we resort to force, guile and deceptiveness to clobber others about.

Sadly, once the source of power and causation is conferred on the so-called "*objective and material*" realm, the power of the mind gets depreciated. No longer being able to fathom the awesome power intrinsic within, we become susceptible to many strange beliefs of the "outside" world. These I referred to also in the Course and termed them '*Magical Beliefs.*' Another unfortunate consequence is that mind-power, once atrophied creates a power vacuum in which feelings of helplessness, vulnerability and victimization kick in. So the dream figure becomes hopelessly stuck in a darkened world context and cannot find the combination to break free. It is a brutal context in which no meaningful questions can ever be asked because one looks only at the screen of effects to provide answers. However, this screen is nothing but a product of our personal ego ignorance. It cannot tell us that it is merely a shadow of our erroneous thought.

"You cannot resolve the authority problem by depreciating the power of your mind."

[ACIM, T-3.VII.2:1]

The only solution for the *'Authority Problem'* is to restore full recognition of your mind-power to your awareness. This encompasses taking full responsibility for the world you perceive. Until then, you will remain conflicted because you will still think "outside" forces have mastery over you. Once you recognize, you made your personal hell; then you will also know where the keys to freedom lie. Your games with God can go almost forever but are all doomed to failure because *"You can perceive yourself as self-creating, but you cannot do more than believe it. You cannot make it true." [ACIM, T-3.VII.4:6-7]* Your only hope is to step out of your game of denial, which is the only mature decision the mind can make.

(Sharon) This all seems to go against the direct evidence of our senses and world experiences. If I went around claiming, that I was master of the entire world of my perceptions, I would soon find myself locked up in the local county jail. Then there might be a psychiatrist trying to put me on Haldol.

(Jesus) Yes, there are a lot of things you are not allowed to question in the Relative World. Anything that probes too deeply at its foundations is considered taboo. As long as you go along with all the charades, you will fit in. As a result, people are allowed to nurse the most outrageous and grandiose self-distortions but are never allowed to uncover their true Identity. They are considered sick if they even hint that there is something grossly wrong with the world. They begin to stick out like sore thumbs and soon lose all their friends. No one is allowed to the universal costume party unless they wear some mask.

Nevertheless, it remains a false and insubstantial world in which cause-and-effect have become horribly reversed. So does the dreamer now appear to be at the mercy of his individual dreams, and has long forgotten himself as its dreamer. Even so, only in his Self-remembering lies any true hope. Yes, he can believe he has accomplished the actual separation from God, but can never make it so.

> **"Your starting point is truth, and you must return to your Beginning. Much has been seen since then, but nothing has really happened."**
>
> [ACIM, T-3.VII.5:6-7]

All your experiences here are but the feverish dreams of a sleeping mind. Dreams that nevertheless have had no effects at all on Truth. You will always remain safe at Home in God's Mind. As you awaken and come closer to Truth, you will see all the maddening effects of this dream entirely disappear. Then you will have no reason to feel fearful anymore. All the illusions and miscreations you saw previously will go up in smoke. For they all only arose from the ego's incapacity to love. Nothing here has the power to stop even a pin from dropping. It remains but an airy chimerical illusion; you were mercilessly beating yourself up with.

Your ill-chosen ego endorsements have proven entirely detrimental to your happiness. They seem to place you in a fearful world of mangled bodies, separation, sickness, and death. One in which you continually engage in meaningless wars and petty conflicts and where enemies seem all about. So you feel your freedom hanging on a gambrel in the slaughterhouse. Hence all the meaningless distractions you pursue. This is the real reason behind all your busy-ness and never-ending '*to-do*' lists. You feel that if you stop for a moment, your enemies will rush in to take advantage. That Truth will devour you! You believe that you will die in Truth, rather than live through it. Who thinks this but the ego! Because *Truth is Life*! There is no Life apart from Truth. All that will happen when your mind becomes un-clouded is that you will be restored to your senses and the seat of your Authentic Being.

The world, on the other hand, is only ever interested in your outward accomplishments. As far as it is concerned, anything that cannot be seen, labeled or quantified does not exist. You see the evidence of this everywhere you go. It is there, in those kids, who are pressured to become overachievers early in life. Very evident also in those cor-porations who prize employees who will work around the clock, while cutting out their home life and interests. So we see a world, in which everyone is quick to point out all their titles, credentials, talents, and qualifications. All their core competencies, experiences, accolades and interests.

Enlightenment, being one of those **"invisibles"** that cannot be measured or seen, is deemed of little unimportance to most appearing in the Relative World.

Yes, there is a living conspiracy around us. All such accomplishments focus and channel all our mental activities into the landscape of the illusory. All our mental action is wasted because our creativity is severely atrophied wherever ambition enters to narrow-band our thought. Nor does this strategy leave any room for the pure and uncontaminated awareness to flower. This can only blossom to the extent that we are prepared to let all the nonsense go. Once you stop reacting to and warring against the shadows of the unreal, they easily disappear from view. Once you stop long enough to reach a quiescent state of mind, Truth will be known. It has always been, but its presence seems masked by all your senseless activities.

THE ART OF NOTHINGNESS

(Sharon) Yes, I see all those distracted self-important beings strutting about everywhere I look. They always seem neck deep in some "critical" pursuits and yet they never seem to be getting anywhere. More like those rats, on a treadmill that are always out of reach of the cocaine. **What antidote do you suggest to all this madness?**

(Jesus) The opposite to meaningless activity is meaningful inactivity. You may call it *'The Art of Nothingness.'*

(Sharon) How does this fine Art, work? Should I just hang out for a few years with all those wasters, lowlifes, and degenerates in their rodent infected crash-pads? Thus gaining that great wisdom that comes from having no motivation and no goals. Is dumpster diving and mooching the path to illumination?

(Jesus) Nice try! No those are real wasters, and they spend all their days either snorting, leeching or sticking needles in their arms. They are pretty lifeless and directionless beings when it comes right down to it. Hang out with those folk long enough, and you will soon find yourself in the gutters and jails of the world, peeing all over yourself.

Then there are those hypnotized by constant busyness. This is their drug of choice. You will find them always nose-diving into some technological gadget or lingering on some social media site. These are the worst poison that faces humanity since they have become almost like machines with their constant flutter of nonsense activity. They may be aware, but they have no Self-awareness. They have what only can be called *'Identified Awareness.'* This is that awareness which extends its tentacles outwards to feast on everything it perceives. So all their information and understanding is derived from their "external" environment. Over time, they become powerless to extricate themselves from the world they perceive and are unable to extrapolate to other domains of knowledge. They are powerless to reach to deeper wisdom or their core essence and have zero comprehension of what they truly Are. No insight into themselves as just a pure awareness. They are unable to differentiate between what is happening and the essence of what they are made of! So most see themselves as entirely defined by their life experiences and the circumstances in which they are embroiled. They live out their lives like puppets on a string and never can figure out whose hand is beneath the dress.

A genuine Master in the *'Art of Nothingness'* exhibits silence, serenity, presence and power. He has given up all futile attachments, desires, ambitions and dreams. As a result, he is simply throbbing with life, spontaneity, energy, and awareness. He had become a flame in the present moment and is always basking in spiritual bliss. Nothingness has become the entire backdrop to his world and being. It punctuates his every word or action, all of which carry tremendous influence.

There is nothing that escapes his attention or fools him with its superficial showmanship or allure. He has penetrated everything through and through — even nothingness itself. He has moved beyond all phenomena, beliefs, and mind-traps that pervade the Relative Existence. His life has become a dance of grace and potency in motion. He is one whose transparent awareness illuminates and enlivens all with the most brilliant effulgent light. When you have accomplished all this, you have mastered *the Art of Nothingness.*

(Sharon) Holy Smoke! This *Art of Nothingness* seems overwhelming and a ton of work. I think I will remain a jack of all trades and a master of none for the present. I have another important question that I have been waiting to ask. **"I did not ask to be Created. Why did God not give me a choice in this?"**

(Jesus) The simple answer is that there was no one to ask beforehand and afterward it was too late. This is the answer that satisfies the ego because the ego fully believes it exists as a separate self and that it has an independent existence. However, from the higher context of the Absolute, this question is seen as entirely meaningless. Because it presupposes some separate "**I**," that was created. Nonetheless, this "**I**" has only ever had a pseudo-existence. That is, it only ever appears in a mind where the illusion of separation rules. It is simply, therefore, an ego question and a product of its ignorance.

In Creation no sense of separation or differentiation has ever existed, nor is it even possible. A mind that comprehends **Totality** sees the ridiculousness of this question immediately. Existence does not ask *"Why do I exist?"* nor does love say *"Why am I loving?"* because it is the inherent nature of existence to exist and for love to be loving. As a Creation of God, you have always existed timelessly. If you had come into existence in time, then there would also have been a time when you were not. Therefore you would not actually exist at all because the Real is eternal. You must simply release your ego notion of your Creation, as some event happening in time.

(Sharon) Since God is all Powerful, why can't He Uncreate me?

(Jesus) You and God have never been separate in any way. Your question is, therefore, asking *"Can God uncreate Himself?"* He cannot uncreate Himself any more than you can create yourself. Absolute power is never Self-destructive. Nor does it possess the power to invalidate itself or its Knowledge. If it could, this would prove that Truth could be destroyed. Truth would then be no different from illusion. Its power and wisdom would be subject to transience and destructibility and its veracity temporal in nature. Since illusions alone would reign, illusions would be truth.

Likewise, if God could destroy Himself, He would be a fearful one. Clearly insane, since what He thought was good before, He would now envision as a mistake that needs to be trashed and recycled. He would be a God that was capable of errors in judgment. None of His Creations would ever feel safe and invulnerable, since they could be relegated into non-existence, on a whim. The belief that God has the power to uncreate is the same foolish idea that light could manifest itself into darkness or love twist itself into fear. Be grateful then of His inability to uncreate you, for it guarantees your safety and Immortal Reality.

FINDING MEANING IN THE DREAM
UNIVERSE

(Sharon) Can this Dream Universe ever be made Satisfying?

(Jesus) It is impossible to be satisfied on a diet of illusions? Everywhere you go, you see the unfortunate outcome of this strategy to happiness. Anxiety, stress, misery, and fear are the inevitable result. Nevertheless, dream figures go about working long hours on tasks they hate just to get some roof over their heads. They buy toys they never get time to play with and engage in numerous tumultuous relationships that have no love at their core. Often they become self-destructive and suicidal, seeing the impossibility of their situation. Their life experience is one of perpetual conflict. The endless clashes between love and fear, mind and body, accumulation and self-aggrandizement versus authentic living.

Forever drinking from this cup of poison, their mortal batteries have become wound down, enervated and flat. So they get to a point where they never even smile anymore, nor can they extend even a single word of kindness. It is not long before they morph into bitter, cynical and depressed psychic-vampires. Human well sippers feeding off any fresh blood crossing into their paths. Some put on bird outfits and jump off perfectly good mountains and call themselves adventurers and base-jumpers. All the same, their sublimated motive for suicide is abundantly evident.

None can look into the mirror and recognize their original face because their connection to spirit has been utterly broken. Divorced from spirit, they cannot clearly think. In their opacity to light, they go about digging through a kaleidoscopic specter of illusions, trying to pick ones to harvest or exploit. So their minds thrash about, like a child with a chainsaw, trying to find meaning where none is to be found. Like Avatars trapped in the confines of a video game, all their actions, feelings, and thoughts are being controlled by the *demiurge.* Their existential angst falls on deaf ears because the video game cannot hear them. Nor can it tell them, that the context in which they appear to live is meaningless. No video game can be a bringer of salvation. It is just a program after all, and all these figures exist just as bits in an IC. Bits that are in constant flux and will completely disappear, once the computer cord is yanked.

Thus it has been, every since that instant of the TMI. We have all been playing this game of an illusory life. Stuck in the matrix of the dream and enraptured by its contents. Even though it is sucking all our thought processes dry, we cannot pull away. Instead, we live off energy drinks and pills and take this image we see in this artificial landscape, to be who we Are. To escape, we must disconnect from our *identified awareness* and search for answers beyond the bounds of the program.

> **"Problems that have no meaning cannot be resolved within the framework they are set."**
>
> [ACIM, WB96.3:1]

So you must find meaningful answers within yourself. You must recognize the insane dilemma that is playing out in your thought. The field of your perceptions may dazzle and tempt for a while — but that is all! It is not going to solve your real problems or bring lasting happiness. Whenever you buy in hook, line, and sinker to this dream universe, you will find only unhappiness. Only when you are prepared to let it all go, will you find real peace of mind! You must come to the realization that you have never been here.

"How else can you find joy in a joyless place except by realizing that you are not there?"

[ACIM, T-6.II.6:1]

This world you perceive only seems powerful, merciless and real to your invented self. For he who denies his Real Identity empowers illusions to reign in their place. However, you can release it all very promptly, merely by recognizing you have never been here. The mirror of the Relative World does not hold you as its prisoner. You are the powerful creative awareness that is projecting all these images and shadows into the mirror of the Relative Existence. Once all your ignorance is cured, you will no longer find a need to project.

GAINING THE MOTIVATION TO HEAL

(Sharon) How can I build up the necessary motivation to heal myself?

(Jesus) You must recognize acutely that illusions will always let you down. It does not make a difference how hypnotizing and seductive they may seem on the surface. Each dream is established on a very shaky foundation and must eventually disappoint. Unless you see the alternative and desire it with all your heart; you will be unwilling to sacrifice your illusions. It all comes down to faith. No one can live without faith in something. Nonetheless, there are only two options in which to invest your faith. You will either harness the natural spiritual strength given to you by your Creator or else place it in your ego self. As long as you believe, you are this dream image and part of the world, you have already chosen the ego.

Deliberate carefully on this! Do you honestly believe your ego is to be depended upon? Will it rescue you at all times? Is it capable of making the right decisions and healing you of fear? Haven't you already seen, how often it has let you down? The ego is concerned, only about appearances and is always focused on implementing superficial solutions. It may dress you in designer clothes and show you off around the town, but it will never heal you at your core!

Resolving your '*Authority Problem*' restores faith in your Creator and is your route to securing real peace of mind. Once you have taken the bold step of acknowledging you have an '*Authority Problem,*' you have already begun to heal. For this is the root of all your problems. Nonetheless, no one can eradicate false ego beliefs while remaining in denial of their Creator because the offshoot of their denial automatically invests their faith in the Relative World. As you begin to make the crucial reversal, you will experience much inner turmoil and conflict. It is all a natural consequence of uprooting the ego and reversing your entire belief system to be in alignment with Truth. As I said prior:-

"As you approach the Beginning, you feel the fear of the destruction of your thought system upon you as if it were the fear of death."

[ACIM, T-3.VII.5:10]

This turbulence is expected! After all, the insidious dynamics of the ego is now being exposed to light. It is likely therefore to become disruptive, if not outright vicious. You have looked at its hand of cards and found them wanting. It was never holding any royal flush — only the jokers in the pack. So for a long time, two opposing belief systems will appear to wage war in your mind. Significant tension and dissent will brew, and some self-sabotaging behaviors are to be expected, as you oscillate between one and the other. Your old belief system is falling away and it will weaken over time because it is fundamentally untrue. However, once you have placed your first steps on holy ground, you will soon find your feet solidly on the path to happiness. Truth will then rush in to release you and give you those treasures your heart has always desired.

There is a place, deep in your heart, that knows it will never be at home in this world. Despite your deep unrest, your own beloved son, the ego, will attempt to convince you it can carve up a safe, joyful and lasting home for you, in this sad world of your perceptions. Jealous of your progress, it will have you bounce around willy-nilly, like some hobo, going every direction at once. So you will walk the boulevard of broken dreams until you finally give up all your ego charades.

The new understanding, I am teaching, paves the way for the ancient Truth to be revealed back into your awareness. Truth, you will want, once you had but a single taste, for no one can uphold this sad world of endless bickering *and fear* and say they are happy with what they have made! A dismal scene it is. One that reflects from every angle all that you have done to yourself, through your ego thoughts! Once you rigorously examine all your beliefs, your only rational and sane choice will be to come into harmony with Truth. Then the sick world of illusion will lose all power over you — because it never had any in the first place. You lent it, all its seeming power, through your belief in it. As you reverse your current understandings of cause-and-effect, you will reenter a meaningful relationship with the Real. You may think that this process will take forever and that you will die beforehand. However, remember what I said before concerning the illusion of death:-

> **"There is no death, but there is a belief in death."**
>
> [ACIM, T-3.VII.5:11]

You have unlimited time to make it Home. However wasting time and vacillating in the Relative World is a much unneeded tragedy. You wait, but upon yourself and your sane decision. Truth liberates all in the end. Nevertheless, it is just a dream of liberation because you are already one with it. A dream of clearing away all fallacious beliefs that you have interposed before it. Your acceleration towards the light depends on your sincere willingness to leave no stone unturned. All crown jewels of your ego need to be sacrificed. All doubt and misplaced trust must be weeded from your heart. Time being neutral, can be used either to help or hinder. You can make more progress sometimes, in just a few minutes of right-minded thought and reflection, than in centuries of linear time.

(Sharon) How can we begin to correct our Authority Problem?

(Jesus) Each should begin by recognizing that they never could create, the miraculous awareness that they Are! For this is a deathless, formless, ever-potent and light-filled awareness, through which all becomes possible. As you grasp what you authentically Are, you will also realize you have a Creator that lies within you. He exists even at a deeper level than your own conscious thought. Rapid progress can be made simply by asking yourself, *"Have I the willingness to see that my brother is not my enemy, but integral to my healing, as I am integral to his?"* Since you both share the same Being, whenever you condemn him, you are also condemning your Self and your Creator. Those whom you alienate become a block to your healing and inhibit the restoration of your Vision. Where there is perfect willingness, no time at all is required because infinite patience yields immediate results.

In contrast, the ego survives by convincing you this landscape of separation is the truth. It whispers endlessly into your ears that you have little in common with others and that your most lucrative survival strategy is to advance through the attack and vilification of another. The ego is like a lone sand bar existing in the middle of the ocean of mind. This sand bar only seems substantial because of the many mistaken beliefs you hold. As you stroll along this sand bar, it is easy to believe you are separate from the ocean. This is, however, an illusion that will not last. It is only a matter of time before your defenses are overcome. Then the vast ocean of Truth will easily flow past them to merge you with itself. You can accelerate this process almost immeasurably by seeing the thought system of the ego, for what it is. One packed with so many artful lies and shameful duplicities that await exposure to the light. Then all reason and sanity within you will yet shine outward, paving the way for Eternal Truth, to be revealed. All problems you currently perceive, reflect past learning failures, and this calls for their correction, nothing more.

Since this ego thought system exists nowhere but in your mind, the correction can be immediate, if you so choose.

Doing so, all illusory effects of the ego will rapidly disappear. You do not have to undo each effect individually because one right understanding can instantly release millions of false images from the screen of perception. Once healed, this thought will extend its healing across inner domains; you could never have imagined. Immediately correcting a multitude of false beliefs that seem completely unrelated. One healing correction has the power to save you eons of time. The closer it is to the roots of the tree of separation, the greater the extent of time obviated by it. Because from each source propagate a multiplicity of other branches, which are simultaneously healed.

You may also wonder, *"How can I ever find truth when I don't know how or where to look?"* The answer is, you don't have to look for truth, it will come spontaneously when you meet its necessary conditions. As I said before, the primary requirement for the revelation of Truth is peace. Peace, you can only have through extending it. *"To have Peace, Teach Peace to Learn It"* [ACIM, T-6.V.B] Truth is already the case. It cannot be manufactured through your efforts. In fact, your misdirected efforts are the only problem. Your Being is already completely immersed in Truth — otherwise, you could not live.

"Knowledge is not the motivation for learning this course. Peace is. This is the pre-requisite for knowledge only because those who are in conflict are not peaceful, and peace is the condition of knowledge because it is the condition of the Kingdom. Knowledge can be restored only when you meet its conditions."

[ACIM, T-8.1.1:1-4]

(Sharon) Unconditional peace seems difficult, almost impossible to ever attain in the Relative Existence. All we find here is continuous change, strife, chaos, unexpected loss and disaster. We are already severely handicapped by not being able to distinguish the real from the illusory, the priceless treasures from the worthless.

(Jesus) As unconditional peace returns to you, the Relative Existence will start to melt and disappear. As your right understanding increases, your consciousness will become vaporous. Then you will be able to perceive the supra-conceptual luminous existence that exists just beyond all your ego barriers. However, If you insist on making peace ambitious, you will fail because once ambition enters, all hope of peace becomes lost. Peace cannot be attained through grasping, but only in letting go! Once you let go of all that is valueless, peace comes naturally on its own. The Holy Spirit will help guide your mind to distinguish the real from the false. Help you to remember the infinitely valuable while discarding the entirely worthless. So will you accelerate rapidly towards Truth!

Realize Truth can never be known as some mere object of knowledge. You know it, through becoming it and merging harmoniously with all that it IS. You already Are it, so this becoming is truly a mode of unbecoming. A removal of all that is false in you. Falsities, that you have unfortunately nourished and identified with since time began. So you are undertaking a journey to remove all unwanted bits of marble. Migrating your consciousness away from that pitiful pile of dust known as the ego, to find the all-powerful, all-encompassing Identity, you never suspected. All great adventures start out with baby steps, but these baby steps soon become monumental leaps. As Emerson once said:-

> *"Sow a thought and you reap an action; sow an act and you reap a habit; sow a habit and you reap a character; sow a character and you reap a destiny."*

THE POWER OF IDEAS

(Sharon) I am interested to know more about the relationship existing between Ideas and Transformation. Can you help?

(Jesus) All meaningful change starts with one sound idea. Where this idea will take you, you can never know in advance. If it is fundamental enough, it can transform your entire living experience. It will most assuredly transport you into the unchartered and unknown. Along the way, you will be renewed and revamped, and your former self will seem such a stranger now. Yes, an idea has the power to take you into an entirely different world and even beyond all worlds.

However, even the most potent and glorious message is powerless to heal or release, if it remains unheard and unassimilated. Authentic living means continuously changing for the good. This obliges one to discard all which is ineffectual and fallacious for that which simplifies and empowers. The Course ideas appear in many different guises. Nonetheless, they all share a single message and content. Each represents just a different face encapsulating one truly radiant and happy thought. The single thought **"Truth**

can never be Destroyed, and Love Remains Forever."
This powerful thought will humble you in the end.

Imbibing it fully into your being and you will begin to feel a powerful and joyful elation. You become more psychedelic and harmonious as your mind is freed from all static, ineffectual and dead patterns of thought. Now like a Kilroy climbing the ladder of transcendence, you are getting ready to peer at the other side. Preparing to uncover the Ark of mystical wisdom, that lay hidden beneath the hollow reeds of the superficial, for far too long. There is a clearly defined process to it all. Ideas first need to be consciously analyzed, digested and reflected upon. At this point, you will be toying with them, like a cat with a mouse. Asking if they are rational, consistent and compelling while also establishing whether they contradict other ideas and beliefs you endorse! Following this, you will need to weed out all excess bias and partiality and determine if they can be quickly put to the test and run through the gauntlet!

Potent ideas have potentially limitless breadth, scope, and portability. They can quickly cross-pollinate to other domains of thought to vitalize and infuse your entire living experience. Sooner or later, they will be seen as inextricable from a far greater symphony! You start to feel as if you are tugging on the entire universe of thought. The important practice is maintaining an open and expansive mind and a willingness to change existing patterns of thought. Not to grasp too tenaciously at the old, if it contradicts the new. We can all have a great fondness for an old coat or pair of shoes, but sometimes we need to move on. To have our wardrobe of thought entirely remodeled and moved out of the '80s.

Now you must turn on your full intellectual radar and be willing to use every mind-tool at your disposal to get to the bottom of things. Begin by rigorously employing your powers for logic, analogy, and reason (deductive, inductive, abductive, etc.) to capture and expose all flaws and inconsistencies. Then exploit your competencies for critical thinking and dialectical insight to spot glaring contradictions. Next, you must put on your deep sea diving equipment and search for all fractures and cracks at the idea's metaphysical foundations. All the dry intellectual analysis in the world can only take you so far. The idea will remain stillborn and powerless to change you unless you are ready to move up to the next rung of the ladder. Intuition can tell you something tremendously valuable is there below. All the same, it is not going to dig it up for you.

The idea can only be made real, through gaining a lasting and abiding conviction in it. Only then, can it begin to germinate and flower in your mind. So you must be willing to test it out in the greater scope of your life. You can start with a small pilot study undertaken in a somewhat lower risk situation. From there, you must progress to a juncture that offers far more exposure. Unless you are butchering some of your sacred cows or purging some firmly embedded notions from your head, you cannot advance in any fundamental way.

Only when you are running into fierce inner resistance and pain associated with the new concepts and understandings, are you beginning to make genuine progress! You must realize, that the most potent ideas will never be found attractive to your ego self. They will run counter to its tactics and go against all its definitions of worth. All Course ideas constitute a belief system that stands in stark contrast to that which rules the ego world. You are learning a new and yet ancient system of Thought. One that is timeless and existed *a-priori* to the world you see. Only this system of thought is capable of undermining the world at its foundations.

Sometimes you need to use a thorn to get rid of a thorn. The new ideas, you are now learning will feel like pure poison to your ego. It will feel the fear of death coming upon it, as this newfound thought invades its turf. It will project its inner anxiety, mistrust, and fear outward to launch attacks upon the Course. Truth, in contrast, never attacks! It merely undermines and relinquishes all that is untrue! It will reveal inconsistencies and inherent contradictions, that can no longer be denied. Remember without your effort; you will never undergo healing transformation and gain access to real peace of mind. To accomplish this, you must become willing to take the ego out.

Most of these ego attacks will be unconsciously motivated. No ego likes to see its sacred cows slaughtered — after all, what will it do for milk now? So it desires to remain empowered in your mind by every means possible! One of its catchphrases, therefore, will be, "*Better the devil that you know than the devil that you don't.*" People live this way all the time. They auto hypnotize themselves into accepting the comfortable lie over the inconvenient truth. It is not an accident that the cloak of bondage is a garment well worn while true freedom is rarely known.

(Sharon) Yes, I have encountered this many times. The resistance to change is mighty in most. Few detect there is an enemy within that is the cause of all their resilience. We all like to delude ourselves with the strange notion, that there is but a single entity behind the screen of our thoughts. One capable of making wise and rational judg-

ments and untainted evaluations. There are two voices inside each, and the ego is unlikely to be partial to the ideas
of Truth. It reacts viscerally to all meaningful change. It
erects a smokescreen of complexity around your mind, at
every possible opportunity and is pleased only when you
are hooked and distracted by marginal issues, of no consequence. That is why most are so closed-minded and un-
progressive. They have developed strong mental blocks to
every idea that interferes with their ego agendas.

(Jesus) Yes, the ego is the decisive reason why most do not
evolve. Even when the only sane choice is hammered out
in black and white, they will still choose the self-
destructive alternatives. It can be so frustrating to watch.
Most are perfectly willing to increase their fear and mental
contraction with each passing year, rather than embrace a
single living thought emerging from outside their tiny domains. Many have developed unyielding and entrenched
learning blocks, even where there is no deficit in their intelligence. Then they proceed to expend considerable energy on flashy distractions and petty indulgences. They
will not spare an ounce of time engaging the new and
transformative.

There is that old saying *"Age is Wisdom,"* but this is rarely
the case. It is far truer to say *"Innocence is Wisdom"* or

"Fearlessness is Wisdom." Age is often just a measure of how stubborn and closed-off, one has become. How poisoned one now is by all the toxins of mental inertia, laziness, and ego complicity. Very often also, you will see young people who are like this. Totally rigor-mortis, incapacitated and overly cautious in their prime. Obsessed about their retirement plans and pension, while still in their twenties.

Each must come to see their ongoing ego vacillations, indecisiveness, and closed-mindedness for what it is — the fear of progress. The decision to hold on to that bag of bones and tattered coat instead of putting on the royal gown of their inheritance. One thing is for sure — the dream will go on indefinitely until meaningful changes are effected. Nonetheless, all meaningful changes are only at the level of the mind. All truly progressive changes in life involve an inward evolution. One must be willing to penetrate all fallacious concepts; one holds dear because each such concept or belief can become the very noose that hangs.

The only revealing understanding within a dream is the one which teaches; it is a dream. With this realization, the real possibility emerges of your imminent awakening. It is one that leads you into the projecting booth and gently releases you from the prison-house that you projected. You come to recognize your true mind-power, as the projectionist. After that, all psychological crutches and false supports soon fall away, and you are transported expeditiously to the never-changing — the zero point of consciousness. Then you begin to see that you have always been the limpid and awake mind beyond all dreams. Just a pure awareness with no content. No longer clinging to illusions, unconditional peace becomes natural and second-nature.

So then, it is only when ideas are experientially tested, that you gain an abiding conviction as to their veracity and potency. Your newly established faith then becomes the principal motivator for continuing to live them out. Over time they become part of your being and entire modus operandi of living. Existential, rather than intellectual. Intellectual analysis, without practice, is just wasted effort. It will soon devolve into just a stream of undigested ideas and a trail of refuse, which litters your path. Unless ideas become existentially tested and embedded within the framework of your life, you will remain unchanged. If you fail to capitalize on all true ideas, which cross your path, you will become lifeless, joyless, and broken-spirited. You will soon lose all tenacity and will. Become merely a flatfish then, on the face of existence. One who can be blown, shaped and twisted by every profiteer, scam artist or proselytizer that rises from that snake-filled cauldron of humanity.

Even if an idea carries all the power of the universe, it remains impotent unless put into practice. Your application of it signatures your willingness to be changed by it. Only then, is its true causal power tasted and known. Powerful ideas are often only hindered by the limited field of applicability to which you extend them to. When you become willing to apply them boundlessly, you come to know their genuine power. For example, when Steve Jobs came up the i-Phone, he wasn't inventing anything new. All the technologies integrated within it had already been around for decades. He was merely putting them together in a new configuration and thus extending their field of influence. Similarly, there are many technologies around today, which when put together in a new arrangement, will make many into billionaires. We call such people visionaries, yet you are holding right now all the ideas you need to enter the gates of Eternity.

So practice brings conviction and universal relevance. The new experiences you reap can often be quite startling. You may, for example, see a physical illness completely disappear, or else experience a deeper tranquility of mind, that you never thought possible. You may find yourself rapidly transformed into an excellent and passionate communicator and able to establish high-quality relationships. Often you will see your every wish and hope manifesting with ease. The impossible has suddenly become effortless. Because whenever you put worthwhile ideas into action, the universe cooperates and opens all its doors.

There has always been a Pandora box waiting for you in the basement of your mind. One you completely ignored and even forgot. One that holds treasures, you cannot even fathom. Once you glimpse the magnitude of the treasures it holds, you will stand in awe. Soon its gifts will be triggering important changes in your life. Freeing you of the Relative Existence and enabling you to look onwards with a joyful and naked simplicity. For you are recognizing now the timeless fragrance and undiminishing potency of all it contains. An ancient spring of hope is bubbling back to life. For you have awoken and broken free of all former restrictions of thought. Fresh air and light are permeating into your dreamworld, bringing to you new life, health, and vitality. All fatigue and weariness will soon be passing away, replaced by perennial bliss and absolute trust in the future. That bleak ego world of fear, madness, and grievances cannot long withstand the gifts of healing, peace, and release that are evidenced now everywhere you look.

UNCONSCIOUS GUILT

(Sharon) Earlier you said that unconscious guilt perpetuates the Relative Existence. This connection isn't immediately obvious. Can you explain in more detail?

(Jesus) Those who appear to live in the Relative World believe it is powered by so many strange laws and unseen entities. The subtle and sometimes mysterious laws of Nature, Science, Medicine and Darwinian survival of the fittest are some prime examples, which I have already mentioned. Then there are all the gyrations of economics, various political policies and all the convoluted codes of the judiciary. Most are firmly indoctrinated early with ego notions of accumulating power through such corrosive means as heartless opportunism, ruthlessness, craftiness, and deception. They believe fully in an external world, riddled with so many dark forces pitted against them. Surveying the immense destruction and madness that prevails, they become desperate to write something meaningful onto this slate — this *Tabula Rasa* of the world. They seek to get an edge, by all means, possible so that they can continue to entertain their illusions of control and even mastery over it. From their desperation and senseless groping, spring all the artificial man-made laws.

Since most cannot see beyond the haze of their personal ego distortions, they are unlikely to self-diagnose guilt, as the sole cause of all their afflictions. No! The real cause of all their perceived ills, grievances and notions of loss is always displaced somewhere else. There is a good reason for this. We see flowers and trees, but we never see their roots. All the same, we know flowers and trees cannot survive without their roots. So it is with the world. We attribute cause-and-effect relationships only to that which is seen. Nonetheless, when a problem runs deep enough and threads every aspect, the roots must become hidden. They disappear back inside the unconscious where they soon become swallowed up and forgotten. Likewise, the Son's denial forced guilt to submerge into the subaqueous reaches of our collective unconscious. Now buried deep below, this heart of all evil remains lost to our awareness.

Meanwhile, the ego uses this world as one of its greatest defenses against Truth. It sees in the world's senselessness, endless bloodshed and callous acts of brutality, compelling evidence that God cannot possibly exist. If it can convince you, that all the world's acts of vengeance, its evil atrocities, and sins are part of God's undying wish for you, then how can He be the Source of infinite kindness and mercy? A God who wills only good things for you? How then can unconditional Love ever be Real? So the ego seeks to smear the Absolute with a very nefarious brush indeed.

Never underestimate the full dynamics by which the ego seeks to survive inside your mind. It will tunnel its ways underground into ever "protected" cubbyhole, cranny or sanctuary, your mind offers. Most of the time, it will go all-out to sabotage your efforts whenever you stumble upon a nugget or two of Truth. Likewise, it has you perennially chasing for answers and solutions where none are to be found. So you head off with your armies of the hopeless, hoping to vanquish the multitudes of enemies seen outside the doorstep of yourself. You never realize the real enemy lies hidden deep within your coconut.

The exclusive cause of all the chaos and insanity is always placed outside yourself. This places you on the fast track to becoming a victim and a patsy in the ego's game of chess. A mere pawn to be tossed aside when the right time comes. It is only when you change the vector of your questioning to probe within for answers, that you have begun to actively threaten the ego's game. It will not tolerate this laser beam shining on it and its foundations and is likely to become outright vicious.

An honest few have recognized they do not understand the world they see, nor the laws by which it appears to operate. Being no longer fooled by illusory effects, these few alone are on the fast path to wisdom. Those poor in Spirit will continue searching "outside" for a meaningful Cause and solution. Functioning, therefore, more like those tramps and vagabonds, who endlessly collect coke cans on the beach, thinking they are heading to the very treasure-house of Salvation. So it is with all worldly and materialistic beings.

You must recognize unconscious guilt as the fundamental bedrock, upon which the Relative World is built. It is guilt alone that provides the foundation and support for its many empires to madness. Guilt motivates all those pretend games of innocence, those self-absorptive fantasy lands, and dreams of specialness, that so many indulge in.

(Sharon) Just saying so isn't going to convince many! Some would say the connection to guilt is tenuous at best and would demand hard proof.

(Jesus) If they were willing to extend forgiveness in place of judgment, they would have all the proof they need. When each looks at the world of their perception, the devastation wrought is so great that the original cause and epicenter can be hard to trace — just like immediately after a bomb explosion. So each feels like a forensic Scientist and tries desperately to piece the evidence together, long after the crime has been committed. Even though the evidence is staring into our face, sometimes it can be hard to connect the dots.

The reality is a great earthquake occurred long ago. However, since its fault-line remains carefully concealed from sight, this fault-line remains denied. Even though the damage above the surface can be often overwhelming, the real cause still seems obscure. This great earthquake was the **TMI**. Out of this poured the lava flows of guilt. This guilt remains the most potent, destructive and ravaging force in our minds. Because it is hidden far below that which the body's eyes can see, its enormous capacity for destruction is often mentally mitigated or altogether disregarded. When you look only at the surface, you perceive a mass army of bodies and forms, drenched in rivers of blood and sweat. All is absolute chaos and delirium and stinks everywhere with the diarrhea of frenzied meaningless activity. Even so, you are still uncertain from where such a world arose.

Blinded by living in darkness for far too long you have begun to impute all sorts of weird cause-and-effect relationships, to the world you see. None of which are true. You are likely to amplify and enliven some of the shadows out of all proportion. That is why I advocated the remedy of quantum forgiveness. Once you faithfully apply this healing antidote to the world of your conscious experience, you will begin to see all the effects of your unconscious guilt rapidly disappear. Then the ego world of hatred and vengeance will fall and be replaced by the Real world of unconditional love and mercy! Through forgiveness, the ego will be vaporized into dust because guilt and the ego are synonymous.

Though guilt has no reality in Truth, it has a very pervasive reality in the split-mind of the Son, who projects the Relative Existence. All notions of guilt arose at the instant of the TMI. Over the eons of illusory time since, this guilt has peopled the world with so many broken figures frantically moving about in it. All made mad with guilt, yet all presenting glowing dream portraits, that declare their innocence. Most are superficial and capable of only living on the surface of the mind. They conveniently ignore all the carnage beneath their feet. They feel if you knew all their guilty thoughts and pleasures, you would disown them as a friend.

So whenever anything happens that invades their peace of mind, they attribute this loss, to causes seen only at the surface. They project it to their jobs, finances, relationships or pure bad luck. At other times, they may attribute their misery to the government, certain elitist factions, to prejudice or even to the village dog. What they fail to recognize, is that this entire landscape was brought about from past eruptions and their underlying fault-lines of guilt.

Often they think they can extricate themselves from all misery, simply by assigning its cause to another. Generally, they pick a carefully chosen target, who is then blackballed with the brush of their innermost self-hatred. At other times, they project this inner hate to another race, religion, gender, social class or belief system. Every now and then, all hell breaks loose, and we have pure pandemonium. We all collectively lose our composure and go to war. It is like a critical mass of our self-hatred gets accumulated and can no longer contain itself. Once the ego games of pretended civility and passive hostility fail, the operation moves from covert to overt. Then because we have all long ago forgotten the great earthquake of 'fore, we do not provide any meaningful or sane solutions.

UNMASKING THE POWER OF THE UNCONSCIOUS

Sharon) Is the unconscious all that powerful?

(Jesus) The realm of the unconscious is the higher order reality. It is far more powerful and aware than your conscious self. Consciousness is the realm of the ego. A domain in which your think yourself separate from everything and everyone. Your unconsciousness, in contrast, operates as pure grace in motion and is faultless in its actions. Take your bodily functions for instance. Are you consciously aware of all their actions? Nevertheless, they perform flawlessly to keep you alive. All this sublime unconscious activity is hidden from your conscious mind and thought. Conscious thought would be an interference. Even were you to look through a microscope and become intimately aware of your cells and their activities, you would still not have the slightest clue how they all work so collaboratively and to such magical precision. There are indisputably tens of thousands of times, in each person's life, when the miraculous workings of their unconscious have helped them avoid a tragic catastrophe.

Even though all the dynamisms and extraordinary operations of your unconscious mind are concealed from your awareness, nonetheless, it is continuously registering all motions of your conscious mind. All your thoughts, memories, feelings, and actions are stored within it where they are linked and encoded in the great unified Akashic field of mind. This field, certain psychics, and clairvoyants tap into often, to access seemingly lost information. Often they use it to solve crimes or to locate hidden or forgotten knowledge.

The activities of the cells of your body may seem like nothing compared to the higher functions of your conscious thought. Likewise is the relationship that exists between your conscious and unconscious mind. The gulf in their level of abstraction and potency is immense. A simple analogy is to consider your consciousness and all its motions, as akin to a straw through which you are sipping on the vast ocean of unconsciousness. Sure, you can get a larger straw — this is what is called consciousness expansion. However, even after spending many lifetimes sucking through this straw, you still know zilch about this boundless ocean and what it encompasses. There remain spacious hidden territories which have never been explored or revealed. The numerous laws, concepts, and beliefs you formulate and extract from your consciously lived experience are comical at best when compared to the almost limitless reaches of the unconscious.

So your conscious knowledge presents a complete distortion and fabrication of Truth. Similar to, the evidence a KKK member would provide, at a deposition hearing for the Dr. Martin Luther King's assassination. As you begin to unravel the full contents of your unconscious mind, you are reaching to the unerring powerhouse that is your key access point to the Real.

(Sharon) I must say, I have had numerous experiences of the power of the unconscious — some could be considered miraculous and others I dare not speak about. I have seen how it has saved my life on countless occasions. Many times I have awoken next morning and wonder how I ever got home safely. How come we do not hear more about the power of the unconscious?

(Jesus) Scientists and psychologists often treat the unconscious, as if it were an inactive and sleeping part of us. In contrast, it is extremely active and always awake. It is that part that never sleeps. It remains fully awake, even in our deepest sleep. Just because we cannot raise all its contents and knowledge to conscious awareness hardly makes it inert. Nor can any even pretend to know all its intricacies and mysterious actions. From this seemingly infinite well, spring all the dynamisms that govern our innate and in-built intelligence. It is the source of all our motivations, vitalities, perceptions, actions, sensitivities, feelings, intuitions, and understandings.

It is your conscious mind that is deeply asleep most of the time. It goes about thoroughly mesmerized and identified with whatever nonsense is going on. Distracted like a kid who can never sit still. It almost never exercises any real vigilance or self-awareness. The unconscious holds many secrets that it can reveal to your conscious mind. To leverage its potencies, you must be prepared to broadband your perspective and become unbiasedly capacious in assimilating new information. You must be prepared to open all floodgates of your mind and shut the jabbering of the little voice up. That inner troll who thinks he is the Wizard of Oz. The unconscious likewise provides an important portal to the hidden dimensions of life. Through it, even experiences of Revelations can arise. Unfortunately, most seek far too much control and cannot let themselves go. They only feel safe living in the picketed white fence territories of the mind. So they roll out the red carpet to welcome in all the *Thought Police* and *Neo-Nazis* of the mind to censor, filter, and band-limit all their conscious thoughts. It is often only after they have gone through some major breakdown or spiritual crisis, that a revolutionary healing breakthrough can occur in their psyches.

It is your conscious mind, that is always twisting your arms into believing its crap. It is forever restricting you to limited and outdated modes of thinking. So it straitjackets and coerces you into getting what it wants while relegating you to old feudal patterns of victimhood, attack, self-pity, and false friendship. It rarely allows you to enter any room; you have never been in before. Only when you have come to resent and detest it with a vengeance, can the tectonic plates of your underworld finally come together!

Only when you come to despise all those carefully manicured pretenses and ideologies floating about in the jungle of the world, are you ready for a quantum leap in your state of consciousness! Then you are ready to vomit up the entire cesspool of existence. Nauseated by all that rubbish, you entertained for far too long, you enter the temple of wisdom and find yourself free. All past thoughts, feelings, and beliefs have now been mercilessly crushed under your feet like cockroaches. All strange notions you cherished regarding your identity are shed like the skin of a snake. It is then that you are catapulted into the stratosphere and momentarily out of the reach of the ego.

(Sharon) Many would quickly disparage all such ideas, attitudes and beliefs, as nonsense and see them instead as a form of Nihilism. Some would say such lines of thought are anything but constructive towards one's Spiritual Development.

(Jesus) Yes, many like to admire their castles of sand and dust. Once anything seems to threaten their carefully chosen edifices to idolatry, they scream "**Spirit is coming quick, let's lock the gates and call in an ambulance for the ego.**"

Nonetheless, let me remind you, Enlightenment only arises out of the greatest spiritual emergency in your innermost core. It is an instant, in which the ego-self is drowned, and you become immersed in the infinite ocean of pure bliss. If you like, we can play some final death march or requiem to give it a sending-off party. Even so, we must not tell it where it is going. Yes, you must rid yourself of that false and limiting self-concept you manufactured, by sipping through the straw of consciousness. See it instead as a pumped up chicken and optical delusion that was always standing in for the Real you! For it was never anything more than an artificial bubble generated out of all your foolish self-obsessions, judgments, and fears.

(Sharon) The vast power of the unconscious is becoming more apparent to me now. All the same, how can I know for sure that unconscious guilt alone exerts such power?

(Jesus) Most often the unconscious is seen as the giant elephant in the room. One to be discreetly ignored and unspoken about. Perhaps you hear a muffled whisper here-and-there, but no one dares speak out loud about the tremendous power it exerts. The ego wants them to feel in control at all times. Likewise, unconscious guilt is regarded as that pestilential presence that has always remained hidden from your sight. This guilt nevertheless established the dark cornerstones from which this Relative World arose. Everywhere are evidenced its insane proclamations and manifestos. It is there in your mass murders, serial killers, terrorist violence and copious acts of self-destruction. It is there in all forms of sickness and suffering. The body and the world are just some pink ribbons over it.

The ego hopes you will never *look-and-see* it for what it is. It does not want you to recognize, that it is guilt alone, that bars you from Heaven. Many other ego beliefs have flowered from these dark roots, to become the trunks and branches of the tree of the Relative Existence. They soon proliferated into numerous corrosive and disheartening forms and make for that vengeful, joyless and meaningless place; you call home. One in which various split-minds and broken bodies go about their lives, thinking their hellish existence with all its problems is somehow deserved and independent of their ego guilt.

Since that unholy instant when unconscious guilt was first introduced into the mind, it has never gone about its business peacefully. The guilt soon became transmuted into a world of judgment, condemnation, and attack. The world of terror and despair arose from the many distortions guilt introduced. Once you rid yourself of all guilt, you can no longer suffer. The ego will never let you admit, that this world of pain, is entirely caused from within. That there alone is the remedy found. It will never teach that this world can never amount to anything more than an outward picture reflecting your inward condition. When you look outwards, you must recognize that guilt alone rules as lord and master in this bleak hall of grim appearances.

It seems Holiness abducted the throne long ago. At that instant, when Creation got replaced by your self-made gods. Consequently, in place of forgiveness, we now see the god of judgment with his blood-smeared lips, forever seeking for more victims. In place of love, there is the ice king of fear, who leaves no room for any compassion, mercy or reprieve. Unconscious guilt rivets deep within us, and the ego is forever clutching at this power gun. It alone perpetuates the false artifice of the separation. Even so, this dysfunctional existence, you consider your finest work of art.

One should not look at the screen of effects for causes. Denial, projection, judgment, condemnation and attack are all mere effects and not causes in themselves. They are all part of the ego's knapsack of psychological dynamics and instituted for its protection. Contractors and minions designed to do all the nasty gut-wrenching work, building and fortifying an impenetrable fortress of guilt around your mind. For the ego aims that you never cross-examine or interrogate your guilt upfront. Nevertheless, these dynamics do all the damage, because they raise your guilt beyond all question. They are the bouncers of the house and accept no guests without a special invite or VIP pass.

Guilt has taken up its residence in the lower chambers. It is forever watching on its flat-screen TVs, all the crimes of the world playing out while lending you its mask of pseudo-innocence. It feels protected because the gates to its chambers are most attentively guarded by the cruel hounds of evil, attack, and sin. As long as you believe these ferocious sentinels have the strength to take you out, you will never enter the inner chambers. However, it is there alone, that you would find your guilt entirely unfounded. All is pure fabrication arising only in a world powered by illusions. Convenient lies and confabulations made to lend these sentinels all their seeming power. Meanwhile, the ego enumerates with such relish all the crimes you have committed to date. Then it strategically deploys its twin dynamics of denial and projection to keep you bound to a profound state of mental dissociation. All the same, this hard coconut must be cracked if you would find its soft center.

No one has ever been able to undo their guilt without first taking these sentinels out. These form the powerbase of all Methuselahs of old. Denial of Truth lead to the great sleep in which awareness of innocence became lost. Your subsequent use of projection causes you to experience yourself as a split-mind. All this resulted in all apparent reversals of cause-and-effect esteemed by the world. So the dreamer became the dreamed and soon forgot his private thoughts caused the multiplicity of evil deeds he sees. These thoughts merely reflect unnatural beliefs needing correction in his mind.

Meanwhile, the ego, in its ambitions for self-preservation has brought about your own destruction. It knows its masks and charades cannot last forever. That they can only deceive children, willing to be fooled. Yes, sooner or later you are going to come pounding at its front door. For it cannot bind you to this dream world forever. As you learn to distinguish its antics from your Real Being, all its motives and goals will become patently transparent. For they always aim to erect and maintain a frozen static boundary between you and others. By disconnecting all-important tributaries to your healing, they seek to guarantee that you will never be released to the wisdom and bliss of Whole-Mind. So the ego invests your days in the search for specialness and special relationships while harshly judging all to very exacting standards.

Having fallen under the hypnotic spell of the dream, you now aspire to give all your guilt away, in a misplaced attempt to purchase innocence. Thus you wander as a hapless victim in a world generated out of your own dreaming mind. You misuse of projection seems to keep you trapped behind the gates of the body. Though you despise it and see it as sinful and wicked, you will not sacrifice this idol made to your ego self. For you still believe it is all you have got. Fearful also, of all the evil deeds you see in the dream, you will not look within and find your Salvation. Hence you feel sentenced to living out a life of a mistaken identity. Finally all those defense mechanisms you instantiated for your protection cement your jailhouse of hopelessness into place. You think you are in Black Dolphin and beyond all hope. Your glimmer of hope fades fast, as you listen more and more to this unholy mouthpiece. For defenses are its protection against the world of light. Without which, all would easily be shined away.

"The world you see depicts exactly what you thought you did. Except that now you think that what you did is being done to you. The guilt for what you thought is being placed outside yourself, and on a guilty world that dreams your dreams and thinks your thoughts instead of you. It brings its vengeance, not your own. It keeps you narrowly confined within a body, which it punishes because of all the sinful things the body does within its dream."

[ACIM, T-27.VIII.7:2-6]

(Sharon) I often wonder how the denied became projected since through denial it was lost to awareness.

(Jesus) Most of your guilt is unconsciously projected. This
has become so habitual and second nature to you now that
it is just like breathing, driving or tying your shoelaces.
Nonetheless, all these actions were once consciously per-
formed before they became unconsciously so. Likewise,
your games of guilt and the various psychodramas you
play out, are now deeply threaded. They have become habitual and instinctive behavioral patterns. Then you wonder why your relationships always breakdown and why
you experience so many communication failures. You most
assuredly believe you do not know! Thus you look out in
innocence, like a child with mud covered hands and face
and claim no part in what has happened.

The projection of unconscious guilt alone led to the world
of separation and the entire delusional system you now
see. From it, fear arose and was invested with all its seeming power to tear your mind apart. Guilt obscured all Creation, and so the luminous radiance of the Real World soon
became lost to sight. Yes, all was covered quickly in a mantle of darkness so dense, that now bodies creep about in it
and shake hands, now knowing they are One.

Fortunately, your Home cannot be destroyed. It exists eternally in light and awaits but your silence in the present moment to reveal itself. Vision will bring it back to you, and you will once again perceive with naked awareness — as Adam once did in the Garden of Paradise. As you voyage deeper, you will pass the circle of fear and expose all foolish beliefs that keep your fear in place. After that, all attraction to guilt cannot long endure. Thus you will have toppled, the greatest hindrance to your Salvation.

"Guilt makes you blind, for while you see one spot of guilt within you, you will not see the light. And by projecting it the world seems dark, and shrouded in your guilt. You throw a dark veil over it, and cannot see it because you cannot look within. You are afraid of what you see there, but it is not there. *The thing you fear is gone.*"

[ACIM, T-13.IX.7:1-5]

YOUR ONLY REAL OPTION

(Jesus) Quantum forgiveness is the dream's antidote to release all unconscious guilt. So is the springtime of hope reborn and memory of eternal innocence floods back to your awareness. An ancient fountain of cure is now bubbling back to life, and the wearisome meaningless journey will soon be over. Now you see, at last, the answer was here all the time. The seeds of guilt that led to worldly descent could not displace your ladder to Salvation. A ladder you are now taking into eternity.

You had ventured so deep into the underworld. However, it was always just a case of, one problem and one solution. Unconscious guilt was the only cause for darkness, as is forgiveness the only bringer of light. Your acceptance of guiltlessness has restored you to vision, and this brings the Kingdom back into sight. Once you acknowledge guiltlessness, the true face of God's Son becomes known once more. Guilt though seeming powerful in illusion, can have no effects on the Real.

A misplaced belief doesn't make for its reality, anymore than an appearance can stand for Truth. Reality has no need to pay homage to mindless ego rants. Every warped thought that enters its distorting mental prism has never been your concern. Its powerlessness becomes evident when you no longer give any credence to its foolish beliefs. Meanwhile, any remaining attraction to guilt will continue to spawn illusionary effects. Nonetheless, the complete healing of the world is just a thought away. You must take the journey to your Source, and see there never was any Cause for guilt. You had spend lifetimes declaring it to be there and yet now that show is over. You can laugh realizing that your Father's love has remained undiminished, throughout all time. Your real existence has always been as a Holy Creation, imaged in his perfect likeness.

THE RECOGNITION OF GUILTLESSNESS

(Sharon) This is all easier said than done. Based on the wacky guilty world, I perceive, it would take forever and a day to heal all the effects of guilt through forgiveness. Can you provide some pointers that may help expedite the healing process?

(Jesus) The first most important step is gaining the necessary motivation. Because unless you glimpse what guilt actually costs you, you will be unwilling to invest any effort to displace it. Consequently, its many witnesses will remain to haunt you! You may ask what does it cost? Firstly, it takes away all hope of happiness and peace and the vision that could set you free. It eliminates all mental clarity and inhibits your natural capacity to work miracles spontaneously. When guilt enters to poison the mind, awareness of your complete invulnerability is lost. You no longer have the ability to communicate inspirationally, with all whom you encounter. Where it is treasured, healing becomes impossible, and you lose access to those Holy instants, which could liberate your mind. Guilt casts you in chains, cripples your health and drowns out all joy. It seems to keep you outside the gates of Heaven while offering no hope of return. So you grope your way about in the dark, not knowing the Kingdom of Heaven is everywhere around you.

Nonetheless, to escape guilt in its entirety, all you need do, is see a single aspect of the entire Sonship without any trace of guilt. Then the true Face of Christ will be revealed to you. Your perfect forgiveness of another will release you. Armed then with compelling evidence of guiltlessness, you will extend this vision everywhere and soon know this alone is true. Yes, the recognition of eternal guiltlessness is your ticket out of hell. The Holy Spirit is your guide on this journey, and He restores to you the vision that heals. As I taught in the Course:-

"Beyond your darkest dreams He sees God's guiltless Son within you, shining in perfect radiance that is undimmed by your dreams. And this you will see as you look with Him, for His vision is His gift of love to you, given Him of the Father for you."

[ACIM, T-13.V.10:5-6]

Dark dreams represent the smoke and mirrors of the ego's thought. The inevitable consequence of viewing through the distortion of an unreal identity. Beyond your many distortions, the truth remains in shining radiance, silently waiting for you, to claim it. As you discard all false knowledge, garnered from your past, you will reach to the illumination of Spirit. Then the inner light of your new-found vision will shine the entire world of form away.

As you progress, past the ego's hall of mirrors, you will reach to the ever-existing and perfect. Be finally empowered to *"Look through the cloud of guilt that dims your vision, and look past darkness to the holy place where you will see the light."* [ACIM, T-13.X.9:6] In that instant, the light of your inner vision will penetrate beyond the paper thin veneer of guilt, that is plastered everywhere on the canvas of

the world. All that seemed to mock and humiliate you before will now be held in check. The realization will dawn
that all darkness existed nowhere but in the past and yet
the past is nowhere. The past you remember merely represents the residual of all ego beliefs, needing to be purged.
Truth has no past, just eternal presence!

All your tenuous associations to guilt arise from the ego's
past actions. Even so, this ego guilt is not yours, and being
time-bound is ultimately unreal. That is why I said, *"While
you maintain that you are guilty, but the source of your guilt
lies in the past, you are not looking inward. The past is not in
you."* [ACIM, T-13.X.4:1-2] Yes, the ego will play many
sneaky games of deception, enticing you to accept its guilt,
as your own. While you see guilt justified in anyone, you
will not find your release. For the ego uses time as its key
defense to cover over your brother's guiltlessness. Nevertheless, his guiltlessness is true now, and you can perceive
it if you wish.

The present moment remains the abode of all healing because only in this silent and timeless dimension can guiltlessness be recognized. As you reach to innocence, all
grievances are naturally laid aside, and miracles of healing
come to take their place. The ego has created a dizzying
array of distractions and defenses to guarantee you will

never see the naked present. It wants you to retain your allegiances to its insane agenda. You may remember these words I spoke.

> **"Guilt, then, is a way of holding past and future in your mind to ensure the ego's continuity. For if what has been will be punished, the ego's continuity is guaranteed ... Guilt remains the only thing that hides the Father, for guilt is the attack upon His Son. The guilty always condemn, and having done so they will still condemn, linking the future to the past as is the ego's law."**
>
> [ACIM, T-13.I.8:6-7; T-13.IX.1:1-2]

Yes, the ego carries a very sickly portraiture of all. One that it continuously counsels you to accept. It is forever scavenging the world of perception, to find more evidence of guilt. For its very survival depends on it. It cannot get enough of this underworld concoction that dulls your senses and removes all clarity of thought. Like some marketing hippy or technological evangelist, it is always ready with its power-point slides, well massaged the night before. All there to present an incontestable picture of your guilt. There is no sacred place where it will not stick its claws, to dig up some more dirt. It is voracious in its appetites and eagerly searches the entire canvas of time for more evidence against you. Like a dog after a bone, it will not give up, until it has sunk its teeth into something juicy. It entices you to defame all and will never let you off the hook until you present some witless victims at its altar. These then become your unholy sacrifices to its god of guilt.

When it is feeling generous and lighthearted, it may say "*I can forgive, but I cannot forget.*" This is merely its euphemism for saying, "*You are done sucker. I have you cooked and firmly under my paws. Just wait and see.*" Because any source of darkness remembered, has never really been forgiven. After all, who can look unperturbed on such damning witnesses from past events and still think themselves innocent? Even so, all these witnesses to your guilt belong to a past, that never was.

"Yet consider this: You are not guiltless in time, but in eternity. You have "sinned" in the past, but there is no past. Always has no direction."

[ACIM, T-13.I:3.2-4]

The case against you is easily dismissed once you make this simple realization. For who can enter into evidence fragments of any unreal dream? Now we see what genuinely makes the ego afraid and so savage in its ways because this statement of your innocence is its complete undoing. It has always been a tarnished and corrupt adviser who mentors through fear, bias, and exclusion. It has remembered nothing holy or good about you. All your acts of kindness were long forgotten the instant they were made. In its mind, all goodness is to be interred with your bones. You must, therefore, call on your eternal guide to wisdom and light in reversing all poor decisions and interpretations made through your ego self. Your Holy guide will reorganize your memory into alignment with Truth and purify your perception, so that you come to witness only the eternal present.

CONSCIOUSNESS AS THE FIRST OFFSPRING OF THE TMI

(Sharon) You said before that consciousness is the realm of the ego. Can you expand on this?

(Jesus) Consciousness was the first direct outcome of the TMI. Before the Son entertained the TMI, the realms of consciousness and perception were completely unknown. The undifferentiated pure, ever-potent and formless realm of the Absolute, alone existed. In this internal dominion, we communicated seamlessly through the One-Mind of God. Love, Bliss, and Creation were all that we ever experienced. After the TMI, the dream of ignorance began in earnest. Consciousness and perception can be considered part of this dream. Part of that, which keeps the Son asleep and drugged in the Holy Garden. As I said in the Course:-

> **"Consciousness, the level of perception, was the first split introduced into the mind after the separation, making the mind a perceiver rather than a creator. Consciousness is correctly identified as the domain of the ego."**

[ACIM, T-3.IV.2:1-2]

Consciousness and perception are not separate. Instead, they represent two halves of a duality. Their relationship is exactly like that which exists between a movie projector and the images projected. Whatever is ideated within must appear without, in forms and pictures that reflect its underlying content. This duality pair can be rightly interpreted as the first direct consequence of Adam's giving in to temptation. The TMI can be construed as the original sin because only after Adam became conscious, could all the other "sins" follow. The sins of arrogance, conceit, pride, specialness, hate, greed, to name but a few.

All the same, Adam's eternal innocence could never be lost because all sin is impossible for a Son of God. The TMI was an unreal thought and all the "supposed" sins, he committed since belong to a spacetime illusion that is not real. Do you sin, if you attack in a state of madness an hallucination born from your impure ego thought? Do you sin if you become greedy for the gifts of illusion, having lost awareness of the immeasurable gifts of Truth? Do you sin, if you dress yourself up in the rags of illusion, and become conceited about your dream image, having lost sight of your immortal grandeur? No! you have merely lost access to your original face and are to be comforted and guided if anything. Seen maybe as an immature child, temporarily lost in foolish fantasies. One in great need of right direction and sound teaching. Thus you can be healed of your temporary state of madness and delusion. One should never attack and vilify another for their miscreative patterns of thought.

Only after the development of consciousness could Adam begin to feel fearful, vulnerable and prone to attack. Before consciousness, the serpent of unconscious wisdom formed a perfect circle of Knowledge. It held its tail in its mouth and needed nothing outside itself. Instead, it represented all Knowledge and all Being. It held no uncertainty and rested on no contingencies. With consciousness, this connection became broken and exposed. So the perfect circuit that kept all illusions and contradictions out was rendered seemingly imperfect. Only when Adam's consciousness evolves again to the point of purity, will the serpent bite its tail once more. In that instant, you will transcend this hall of ignorance. Then all meaningless questions will come to an end because a state of enduring certainty will have been reached. All worldly questions arise from the ego, who can know nothing for sure.

Hence the Son's embryonic and persistent desire for specialness resulted in consciousness and perception. Consequently, he entered the realm of split-mind in which illusions and false understandings first appeared. Before this, evil was entirely unknown. Evil can be tacitly understood as the direct result of operating under the ego's control and direction and it goes against all life and progress. There is no evil apart from the ego and both are non-existent in Truth.

Original Mind does not experience the realms of con-sciousness and perception because that Mind transcends all duality. It, therefore, contains no impurities by which illusions could propagate. In Original Mind, male and fe-male are perfectly integrated together, and so they time-lessly remain. The animus and anima when wholly fused, function flawlessly and harmoniously as One. When Adam fashioned Eve, from one of his ribs, this signified the de-velopment of split-mind and the apparent separation of the male and the female. To this day, this continues to show up as bodies of both sexes appearing in the Relative Existence. Nevertheless, at the instant of your Enlighten-ment, you will once again witness your inner male and fe-male fuse into a single Being. This is an integral part of the monumental healing of your split-mind, that occurs at this holy instant. Even so, this marriage is only happening at the level of illusion because in truth they have always been joined.

THE WORLD AS A PRODUCT OF YOUR BELIEFS

(Sharon) You keep saying, that which is ideated within must appear without. To me, this all sounds like the most excellent and ultimate form of justice, but I would like to know more.

(Jesus) The world has never been independent of you and your beliefs. All that you perceive and experience is but the creative manifestation of all your beliefs. You are shaping the world continuously out of a sea of infinite potentialities. All becomes adjusted and remolded to meet your instantaneous learning needs. All chaos, contradiction, and false appearances you witness arise from your ego projections and choices. The world will appear ugly or beautiful depending on your state of mind. You are the creative artist who fashions the picture, that is being perceived. Perception always appears fresh each instant, in perfect correspondence to your beliefs.

When you use the world merely to serve your private interests, it will seem to exploit you. Attack it, and you will retreat in fear. See evil forces in it, and you will feel victimized. Show it love and compassion, and it will shower you with kindness, gratitude, and healing. Give it all that you have and Are, and it will repay you handsomely with interest. Arising entirely out of the intricate nexus of your thoughts and feelings, it gives you each and every moment exactly what you deserve. You cannot be unfairly treated by the world because it always gives in perfect reciprocity to your individual gifts to it.

This transcendent understanding will release you, in the end. It is the reason I have said in the Course that "*Perception is Learning.*" Once you faithfully apply this understanding universally, you will no longer feel like some neutral Patsy or "Victim" sitting on the fence of existence. Instead, you will recognize yourself as this world's empowered architect and designer. Yes, a new potent understanding will have dawned to your awareness. That there is no observer and no observed, just the process of creative observation. All that every happens here is the picturing back of your thoughts and feelings, in various images and forms you can relate to. For it is but a blank slate that receives all your belief impressions. This space has no real existence and merely serves as a basis for learning. All notions of dimensional spaces are pseudo and just reflect improvements in your psychic-evolutionary capabilities. You are always the dreamer of all that is perceived and the one that gives all its meaning. The world will always reflexively picture back the primary content of your beliefs.

Perception is not Reality. Reality is beyond your individual making and beyond all belief. It is based on the Laws of God, as established in the beginning. Eternity is in your Mind. Nonetheless, the Real world cannot be perceived until your mind is extensively healed. Until then, nothing can be said which would make any sense using the symbolic terminology and concepts; you are presently aware of. You cannot witness the Real world while you continue to interpose a world of fantasy before it. Your fantasies and erroneous beliefs function as a darkened overlay that block direct experiencing of the Real. Your perception will be automatically purified and become luminous once you attain to right understanding.

By steadily and consistently canceling out all effects of the TMI, from the screen of your perception, the Real world comes into view. Then you perceive the glorious and true existence that lay beyond all your false beliefs. By extending veracious understandings from your mind, the Holy Spirit restores you to the vision that shines the entire world away. Then you know, you have always been at Home in God, and find yourself enveloped and immersed in the radiance, luminescence, and perfection of true Being.

THE TMI AND THE BIG BANG!

(Sharon) We appear to be living in a world these days that is riddled most pervasively with various objective belief systems. Theories, like the Big Bang, Genetic evolution, Intelligent Design, etc., all have been given higher precedence than spiritual theories of its Creation. Everywhere we go, we are bombarded with exotic New Age sounding terminology. Words like naked singularities, wormholes, event horizons, multiverses, polymerase chain reactions, morphogenetic fields, etc., are on everyone's lips. **Is there any truth to all these modern theories?**

(Jesus) All egos like to have their Big Bang theories and endless firework shows. After all, the ego itself only came into seeming existence with the Big Bang of the TMI. It was only after this, that the Relative World of spacetime first appear in the mind. Even so, it will never amount to anything more than an illusory effect of the TMI. A mind-made artifice decorated and adorned to precision by the ego. Another consequence of the TMI was the first appearance of dualities. The dualities of **consciousness-perception** and **male-female**, I have already spoken about, but there are many others. Other dualities include **(i) Ignorance - the**

Relative Existence (ii) Mind - Matter and **(iii) Illusions - Split-mind**, to name but a few.

The presence of these dualities and the ego's split-mind mode of operation are synonymous. A mind that is fully enlightened and healed has transcended all such dualities. It therefore no longer experiences the illusions of split-mind. Since the TMI is an idea, incapable of being shared with God, it is not part of the fabric of Reality. It is therefore utterly powerless to destroy Truth, yet it is completely devastating to your awareness of Truth. Belief in its many effects is the greatest obstacle, to your attainment of real peace of mind. Until you recognize fully your complete dependence on God and the unharnessed capacities of your mind, you will believe many of the TMI's effects are powers in themselves. The plan of Atonement will, therefore, be rejected. Many things came about at that instant of the TMI, including:-

(1) Lost awareness of Knowledge, Innocence and Whole-Mind
(2) Development of Split-Mind
(3) Birth of the all ego beliefs (including the apparent separation)
(4) Fear

(5) Judgment

(6) Miscreation and Illusion

(7) The Need of Learning and Learning Devices such as

       (i) Space-Time (ii) Consciousness-Perception

(8) The Need for Miracles and Atonement

(9) The Holy Spirit

The modern scientific theory, unfortunately, is the belief that objective existence is a bonafide reality. It teaches that mind is a consequence of matter, instead of its cause. That we are appearances in the world, rather than the world is an appearance in our consciousness. It does not recognize the awesome and limitless power of consciousness and mind. Consequently, it reverses monstrously authentic cause-and-effect relationships.

OUR NEED OF LEARNING

(Sharon) You just said that our need for Learning was one of the many consequences of the TMI. Can you explain further?

(Jesus) Before the instant of the TMI. Adam possessed perfect Knowledge. After it, his Divine Knowledge remained intact, but unfortunately, illusions were added into the mix. It is these illusions alone that keep Truth from our awareness. Thus we remain perpetually confused, about the world and our true Identity. Adam, in his drug-induced sleep, needs to make crucial breakthroughs before he can restore back awareness of his original perfection. The process involves identifying and eradicating all that is false in the mind. It is an intense training program to weed out all inconsistencies and to reverse all misplaced understandings of cause-and-effect. He must transcend all dualities and overcome all contradictions. Only then, can he know himself as he has always been! This process is that of self-purification and through it one's purpose becomes clear. The 365 lessons, I gave you in the Course will be of great help since they constitute God's plan for your Redemption and Salvation.

Imagine all incorrect beliefs and inconsistencies in your thought, as being placed in a bucket called wrong-mindedness. Now visualize all correct understandings in a bucket called right-mindedness. Once you have cleaned out the bucket of wrong-mindedness, something truly incredible happens. With no vestiges of the ego thought remaining, all illusions are erased, and the entire landscape of perception disappears. It is at this critical moment that God takes the final step which lifts you up and restores you to Knowledge. Then you become completely aware of the Kingdom and of nothing else. Then the bliss of your perfection and power is all you know and experience.

In the meantime, all your choices and decisions will determine whether you are making progress or not. They determine whether you are reaching to perfect knowledge or else falling back into the hellish nightmares of the ego.

THIS WORLD IS ESCAPED THROUGH TRUTH

(Sharon) You have said that this world is not escaped by death, but only through Truth! This sentiment was also spoken of in the Course. I have provided your exact words below for reference.

> **"The world is not left by death but by truth, and truth can be known by all those for whom the Kingdom was created, and for whom it waits."**
>
> [ACIM, T-3.VII.6:11]

I find this statement both fascinating and revelatory. I would like to know what are some of our principal obstacles to attaining Truth?

(Jesus) The only obstacle is your unwillingness to give up all false beliefs. There is a great reason for this — your enduring investments in the ego. The ego lures you in through various temptations and then convinces you that giving all your hate and guilt away is the means to purchase innocence and happiness. Naturally, it advises that the best way to protect yourself is by attacking and undermining others. Likewise, it teaches one can gain only through another's loss. All of this seems far more attractive than accepting all the guilt, evil and hatred you feel are your own. Unfortunately, this scheme doesn't work because they are your own. They are products of your ego and your subscription to its network of beliefs. Nevertheless, the allure and distortionary power of these ideas keep you hypnotized and therefore unwilling to question them. Soon inertia sets in, and you devolve into old familiar patterns. Dead patterns of thought that offer no hope of healing or release.

You must realize that all obstacles to light are mind-made. Train your mind then to reject everything you are taught, unless you know it to be true firsthand. In this world, you are incessantly flooded with useless ideas and information. A multiplicity of nonsense messages that do not change you an ounce. Shallow ones that merely confuse you or send you on divergent paths, leaving you dull, unhappy, and mentally clouded over. Hence, each idea you accept must have proven its merit to you, through being rigorously tested and analyzed in the fires of your experience. For only thus can it gain an abiding conviction in your being! That is why Socrates said, "*The unexamined life is not worth living.*" Only the examined life takes you on a meaningful adventure towards truth. Otherwise, you are just bobbing about in the ocean of existence, falling deeper into its hells.

The shortage of good information has never been the problem. It has always been in your filtering apparatus. How do you reliably distinguish and separate the good from the garbage? How do you test and expose the veracity of two conflicting messages? Can you unmask the true content of an idea and assess its potency? Do you know its bloodline and family tree and all ideas related to it? It must be evident that ideas do share genetics and most often are just many different faces circling the same content. Learn to look beyond the particular and see the more generalized form. This will help you to distinguish its true content.

(Sharon) Could you provide an example of this approach?

(Jesus) Compare the difference in the following two statements. "*Elizabeth is an evil person*" and "*All people are evil.*" The generalized content of both messages is identical because both are stating evil is true. If you dislike Elizabeth, however, your are probably far more likely to embrace the first statement than the second. The first seems reasonable and enticing, whereas the second can seem preposterous and absurd. Reasonable or unreasonable to whom, you might ask!

To the ego of course! The ego always attaches itself to specifics, in the hope that you will swallow all its mind-poisons and not overly scrutinizing them. It is always twisting your arm with specifics — bribing you on your weak spots. Once you have consumed the content it is selling; it has won the game of dominance in your mind. Because if you are capable of seeing one person as evil, you will quickly project this belief to others and alternative situations. Suddenly, you will find yourself surrounded by a thoroughly evil world. Nor will you be able to escape the picture of seeing yourself as evil in the end.

All the time, you would never have accepted the more generalized message that "*All people are evil*," if you knew the destination it was taking you to — a world of evil inclusive of yourself. Likewise, it is with all the ego's messages. They are all nicely packaged into tiny little parcels that you find easier to digest and manage. One day it gets you accept that "*Elizabeth is evil*" and the next that "*Kyle is Sinful*," "*Jones is guilty*" and "*Lucy is nothing but a broken down body.*" Soon you are saying "*All Gays are Sinful*," "*All Evangelists are Guilty*" and "*All women have inferior Bodies.*" It is not long before it has sold you on all its dark cornerstone beliefs and ideologies. You find yourself going about, reflecting silently to yourself *"All people are guilty, evil and sinful and nothing but broken down bodies."* Nor can you contest this anymore, because you compromised your position by buying in, in the first place.

Then it carefully scavenges perception, searching for more whom you dislike, to strengthen its case. So your dragnet goes to work once more in the swamp of the world. Soon you are given free reign to project the ego's self-preserving thoughts to anyone who falls temporarily or permanently out of favor with you. One day you wake up and find yourself surrounded by a world of evil, sin, and guilt. One in which everyone is miserly and corrupted and only out for themselves. You long for the innocence and idealism of your youth, but it seems trust is no longer justified. Instead, all those hate-filled judgments you projected to the screen of the world come back to haunt you. Soon you find yourself isolated behind a network of self-made defenses, afraid of everyone that walks and breathes.

There is no doubt that evil, sin, guilt and bodies are very evident in the world of your perceptions. Denying this would be an extremely counterproductive form of denial. However, you need to probe deeper and see exactly how all this precipitated. Firstly, it is solely your investment in various forms of ego nonsense, that keeps you bound to the Relative Existence. The Relative Existence reflects the ego and its many strange beliefs. Your continued belief in evil, sin, guilt and bodies drive all these appearances in the world of your perception. Thus you create a living hypothesis in which your core beliefs produce the actual effects that reinforce their message. Atonement is here to wipe all such madness from your mind. Atonement's key feature is forgiveness.

Atonement recognizes how deeply enmeshed you are to this ego world and your complicity to all its beliefs. It sees all the temptations and idols, you prize and all the man-made gods you have erected. It knows that all ego beliefs will soon find evidence and witnesses to testify on their behalf since your mind is very powerful in producing evidentiary effects for all that it believes. All, of which can be easily undone when you no longer blindly accept the distortionary, biased and fallacious. For all mental phantoms are recognized to be insubstantial when interrogated up close.

In the end, either God is real, or the ego is — both cannot be true! Both offer mutually exclusive interpretations of

the world you appear to live in and of your exact relationship to it. Once you embrace only those understandings
that are in harmony with truth, will the Real world reap-
pear back into view! For it is **Here-Now** silently waiting
for you. It remains unperceived because of the blindness of
your ego beliefs. This unholy nexus of mind spaghetti you
have entertained since the instant of the TMI.

**(Sharon) The ego is forever coming up with weird sug-
gestions and interpretations. It is constantly on the
prowl. How can I spot it and foil in its ways?**

(Jesus) You need to take it out on its own turf. That is, in
the world of specifics. Whenever it tempts you with such a
ridiculous statement as *"Elizabeth is evil,"* you immediately
apply the counter-measure of stating *"Elizabeth is not evil
because evil has no part in Truth."* You can inhibit the ego
by changing your mind on specific thoughts. Once you succeed in an individual case, you will soon learn how to extend this power to release all people and circumstances.
Then the light-filled messages diffusing from your mind
heals the entire landscape of your perception. Remember
your mind is incredibly powerful. Never casually disregard
anything your think, because there are no idle or neutral
thoughts. Each can be tremendously lethal or conducive to
your healing.

Changing your mind on simple things is pivotal to your Salvation. As you return to sender, all beliefs you attempted to project before, your world begins to heal. No longer projecting guilt, a miraculous transformation occurs within, in which you immediately glimpse the complete justification for forgiveness. No longer attempting to give your pain away, you find it was never real in the first place. The myth of its existence was always being substantiated through your use of projection. By forgiving others, you forgive yourself.

Thus you come to know that guilt has no real power and no foundation in Truth. All its effects are easily undone through the wisdom and light of the Holy Spirit. A moment occurs when you see the naked unblemished innocence of all Creation. It is a glorious moment in which you find you are no longer alone. One in which you fully recognize the source of your healing is everywhere. These broken ones you misperceived before, were always carrying the cure for all your pain and self-hate. You would never accept their gift because your dream of specialness kept them at bay. A simple change in direction in the arrow of your thought was all that was needed.

In stark contrast, the ego's plan is to first establish the world of sin, guilt, and evil as real and then attempt to rectify the situation. It is always making a false show of humility. This is why it endlessly placates you with various euphemisms and tells you what a swell guy you are. The better man for sure! One that can remain undaunted while looking at the full testament of another's guilt. One who can peer into the very face of evil and not avert his eyes. One who can withstand the callous spectacle of another's wickedness and sinful atrocities and still forgive. Nonetheless, once you have made any source of darkness real, you will be too fearful to uncover the spiritual light that releases all.

"You cannot dispel guilt by making it real, and then atoning for it. This is the ego's plan, which it offers instead of dispelling it."

[ACIM, T-13.I.10:1-2]

So the ego's strategy calls for an endless array of energy expenditures, attacks and false shows of forgiveness. Its ultimate goal is to prove guilt is real and then attempt to forgive it. All the time, it is thinking slyly to itself, that this false show of forgiveness is wholly unmerited. One cannot cure a headache if there is no head. It is simply your belief that there is guilt, that is the cause of all your troubles.

"The purpose of Atonement is to dispel illusions, not to establish them as real and then forgive them."

[ACIM, T-13.X.6:6]

The ego's approach is very much anti-life. It demands complete proof of Heaven before it will allow you to make any sacrifices of the unreal. All the same, it is because of your failure to make such "sacrifices" that you do not know Heaven. You perceive only the imaginary and can never get a glimpse of Heaven — even though it is shining in silent benediction of peace all around you. The ego is like the cautious skydiver, who will never jump out of a plane unless it is 100% guaranteed of a safe landing. Never jumping, you miss out on all those mind-blowing experiences that could have vigorously transformed you. Instead, you get stuck in various safety algorithms, contingency plans, and divide-and-conquer approaches. For the ego has no trust and faith in people, or even in life itself. That is why it is always breaking situations down into more manageable pieces. So it takes a few figures to the side and attempts to twist and commandeer their thought to be in line with its personal interests.

My approach has you take the plunge first, then you can think about it as much as you want. Yes, you can hem and haw all the way down, if you like. I know, with certitude that once you practice true forgiveness, miraculous trans-formations will occur and fortuitous events will begin to transpire in your life. Existence will bestow all manner of gifts to you for your little token of faith in it and in those around you. As you become healed and released, you will want to do it even more. Soon even the happy dream is over, and you take the quantum leap back into eternity.

You must deny the world of appearances wherever it con-tradicts the truth of love, peace, and eternal innocence. In-stead, actuate the Real into your awareness and begin to taste your true Inheritance. As your split-mind becomes increasingly reintegrated and healed, you begin to work miracles more profusely. Then one day, you find yourself completely illuminated and realize your mind was never split, but always Whole. All those erroneous ego beliefs you endorsed merely created the illusion that it was hope-lessly fragmented. These alone lead to your profound state of dissociation. Now as you emerge and bask in your newfound holiness, you realize the path to truth and glory was always right in front of you.

(Sharon) Is forgiveness the only way to return to Truth?

(Jesus) Forgiveness is the way of the heart. By bestowing that which the world will never give, you become healed of all beliefs in guilt and sin. Thus you come to know of your unalterable wholeness and abundance. Forgiveness is the insecticide and weed killer for the ego. As you begin to forgive, the ego can no longer survive in your mind. Instead, its powerlessness and complete lack of veracity become self-evident. You recognize now that you blind submission to it had held you captive for far too long. That your subservience blanketed your world in darkness.

The relinquishment of all false beliefs can also be effected through the path of reason — this is the way of the head. By probing deeply into the metaphysical foundations of the world, you come to know of the illusory nature of time. In a moment of revelations you recognize the **Eternal Now**, alone is true. Investing your trust in the present, you become released from the world of appearances. Relinquishing past and future, you become restored to vision. Then you enter a life of grace and ease and become totally relaxed for the first time. Available to the Holy Instant. Only those who have gained complete trust and confidence in the present can be said to be truly alive. They are invulnerable to the ego because all its temptations, dreams and empty offerings can no longer entice.

When you are no longer hypnotized by idols or seek for retribution on the past, you have found the ego out. Seen it is the perennial flimflam man, who has always come up empty. One that has perpetually swindled you out of your true inheritance. Finding your peace and contentment in the everliving present; the future becomes released. The future your mind now generates becomes open-ended and unbounded since it is no longer being shredded by all your idle ego scripts. No longer contaminated by all its unnatural wishes and wants. Finding all your needs met in the present, you become open to experiences of revelations. Then God communicates directly to you.

The path of reason is powerful and fast only for those who are impartial, rigorous and honest in their questioning. Efficacious for those ready to expose all errors now so that truth can be revealed. This path will be difficult for those with deeply set egos and twisted minds because their ability to reason rationally will be too fogged up by their contemptible ego investments. This path of correcting error through reason can rapidly bring one into harmony with the Knowledge of Spirit. It was this path; I was referring to when I said:-

> **"Truth cannot deal with errors that you want. I was a man who remembered spirit and its knowledge. As a man I did not attempt to counteract error with knowledge, but to correct error from the bottom up. I demonstrated both the powerlessness of the body and the power of the mind. By unifying my will with that of my Creator, I naturally remembered spirit and its real purpose."**
>
> [ACIM, T-3.IV.7:2-6]

Therefore never emphasize error, because what you teach, you will learn. To focus on error is to teach it has reality and power and this will lead you astray. It is wise to never correct another, but rather to emphasize their sanity and strength. After all, who are you to judge and correct those, whom God Created perfect? As I said in the Course, it is always more sagacious to never attack another's position, but rather to protect the Truth. Not that the Truth needs any defense, but your vigilance on its behalf restores it back into your awareness.

Your ego being self-righteous will always seek to correct another and often preach of its own superiority in this process. Any imperfection you perceive merely reflects your own ego interpretations of their actions. Who are you to undertake the correction of another when you are un-healed yourself! Were you healed, you would not see their mistakes but recognize instead their holy light! That eternal spirit within that remains forever flawless and pure.

Likewise, when you focus on guilt, you are attempting to teach of guilt's ultimate reality. Your futile attempts at its displacement through projection do not remove your belief in it. They merely represent the futile attempts of your ego to circumvent a problem by denying its real source. Your misdirected attempt to displace it then guarantees it will not be resolved. Because only at its Source in your mind, can it ever be released. This sentiment is echoed many places in the Course. Here is one such example:-

> **"Those whom you see as guilty become the witnesses to guilt in you, and you will see it there, for it *is* there until it is undone. Guilt is always in your mind, which has condemned itself. Project it**

not, for while you do, it cannot be undone."

[ACIM, T-13.IX.6:6-8]

Just as you can never quench your real thirst by drinking water from a mirage, so you can never heal your ego beliefs by seeing another as the aggressor that fuels them. Your real thirst will remain within until there it is quenched. You cannot vanquish your inner sufferings and feelings of guilt while continuing to perceive "others" as guilty and sinful and beyond all redemption. God's Son is One, not many. You have been reminded of these doomed ego mechanics so many times before.

"It is inevitable that those who suffer guilt will attempt to displace it, because they do believe in it. Yet though they suffer, they will not look within and let it go. They cannot know they love, and cannot understand what loving is. Their main concern is to perceive the source of guilt outside themselves, beyond their own control."

[ACIM, T-13.X.3:4-7]

MIRACLES

(Sharon) I must admit, some of your teachings on miracles can be hard to digest. For example, you have stated miracles happen all the time and that there is no order of difficulty to them. Still, often miracles seem no*where*, to be found. If anything, curses, mishaps, and tragedies are rampant in our world. There appears to be no limit to the damage these inflict on our peace of mind. I think most of us have had the privilege and pleasure of having an addict in our lives at one point or another. Often a veritable Anti-Christ in motion. Someone who sabotages us again-and-again and parasitically consumes all our free time and emotional resources. After some years, the psychological scarring can be extensive.

Then there are others, who expend all their resources into a business only to see it go bottom-up while they fall further into debt. Often their ideas and strategies are fundamentally sound. They just required an opportune boost, that never came, since they were not celebrities or lacked political muscle. Often after trying another, they just witnessed the same process repeat. Then there is the interview trail of tears, which definitely seems rigged in favor of certain types. Minorities know that it is only too real. Experience and creativity often mean nothing if the inter-

viewer feels threatened by who you Are. Some will sabotage you in the interview by asking questions designed to
guarantee you fail or look incompetent. Where is the miracle under such circumstances?

(Jesus) Miracles are instantaneous, but they cannot work
against important life lessons. Experiences are needed for
one to heal and be transformed. Nevertheless, the particular struggles one has to deal with will be different for each.
Some have all the cash in the world but cannot find any
love and connection. Others are fundamentally different
which brings them experiences of alienation and mistrust.
Their isolation however is needed to enable them to blossom since their raw purity would be contaminated by pa-
rochial influences and the mediocre mind. Certain "expo-
sures" force one to adjust their destructive thought patterns, poor interpretations or feelings of victimization. Yes,
the temptation for immediate gratification can be great,
but indulgence and reward where there is no progressive
change, would rob you in the end. You need to know the
effulgence and self-sufficiency of your true being. The miracle is not here, like a good fairy, to grant you all your ego
wishes. If it did, you would rapidly become wasteful, indul-
gent, dissipative and dull of mind. Squander all your time

and opportunity and be perfectly content to stay in the relative existence indefinitely.

Instead, misery and suffering can be the greatest bringer of change. It can press you to scrutinize the real roots of your pain so that these can, at last, be laid bare and dislodged. Often these roots are heavily masked and hidden through denial. Once you come to see, that all your pain is the direct result of your many ego-investments, you are making an all-important shift. Then you recognize also your failure to connect to spirit and that this is your self-imposed block to finding true happiness and peace. Happiness cannot come from demanding more from a world of illusions, but only in reaching to the real. It is found only by those who cling to no illusions. Your many superficial attachments are one of your greatest poisons binding you to the world of pain.

(Sharon) All these things are easy for you to say! After all, you are nice and snug in Eternity. Feed all that propaganda to those VETs who get blown up each day with IEDs. Tell them how miracles are instantaneous and profuse, as they frantically search for their limbs in the innumerable snakepits of this world. Then as they pull out of their foxholes, broken spirited and unable to focus, maybe you can sing to them lullabies of this being an important life lesson.

(Jesus) Everyone is at Home and snug in Eternity. Some of us are aware of it — that is all! The whole aim of the Course is to restore this awareness. All who have found lasting peace had to go through the hell of the world and decrypt the real source of their misery. Yes, there can be no Enlightenment unless one has become stripped naked and bare. Purged of all foolish dreams and temptations and worthless attraction to idols made of dust. I understand some of your resentment and cynicism. You helped a veteran for many years, who turned out to be a cutter.

(Sharon) Yes, and all the time I was waiting for some miracle. Eventually, it showed up but only after enduring seven years of stress, anxiety, and pain — not to mention numerous calls to 911.

(Jesus) The miracle couldn't come before that because you both needed to heal. It was vital that you strengthened your capacities as a healer and displace the underlying cause. Then one day you did. You recognized that the cutting was just a symptom and you were able to teach him of his underlying wholeness and perfection beneath his host of symptoms.

(Sharon) You say miracles cannot interfere with valuable learning lessons. However, you also teach that everything that seems to happen is a crucial learning lesson. Your exact words were *"Perception is Learning."* Your convoluted rhetoric therefore pretty much renders all miracles null and void.

(Jesus) You are right in what you say. The miracle has always been an effect and never a cause. An effect of making the right decision and choosing with the Holy Spirit. No miracle can ever be the result of choosing with the ego. Wherever you seem to find yourself in the relative existence, it will be a learning lesson. The real question then is whether you are going to choose with the Holy Spirit or with the ego. This decision determines if you will witness a miracle or not. You may remember these words below from the *Principles of Miracles* section of the Course.

> **"Miracles are thoughts. Thoughts can represent the lower or body level of experience, or the higher or spiritual level of experience. One makes the physical, and the other creates the spiritual."**

[Miracle Principle 12]

I also taught that *"Miracles are everyone's right but purification is necessary first."* **[Miracle Principal 7]** Most do not understand what the process of purification is. Hence they cannot reliably produce the miracle which is their God given right. All the same, they seem perfectly competent and proficient at using guns. Purification simple means getting the ego out of the way so that all your decisions are in harmony with Spirit. Unfortunately, most think almost exclusively with their egos. That is why their lives are such disaster zones. Why they are continuously self-absorbed, selfish and ruthless in their behaviors and their minds too contracted with dark mental patterns to ever distinguish the light.

(Sharon) This all brings up another important consideration — our collective need for purification. It seems there is an ongoing trend in our society, to consider all random massacres, bombings, and terrorist activities as the work of hateful fringe groups or isolated psychotic individuals. Thus it seeks to conveniently sweep all its own ills and responsibilities under the carpet. Even so, I can't help feeling something deeper needs to be faced. That the lone wolf strapping 100lbs of TNT to his back, ready to blow away the competition, is in many ways a direct product of our society.

(Jesus) True, hateful fringe groups do not grow in a vacuum. Often they are the result of certain inequalities and injustices, which have gone on unchecked for far too long. The essential underlying dynamic is collective projection because society likes to demonize and alienate certain groups to cover up its inherent lack of love and failures of inclusion. One of my fundamental teachings is that *"All thought is shared."* No one is ever alone in experiencing the effects of their ideas and beliefs. There will always be consequences both for yourself and others from every decision you make. Similarly, all healing is shared, as are all its effects. One cannot and does not heal in isolation. Either society will heal collectively, or it will not heal at all.

As for those lone wolf individuals who commit such monstrous atrocities, the same inner emptiness and alienation is often the underlying motive. No one who feels happy, included and loved commits such horrendous acts. It is all too easy to label them as psychotic freaks acting alone. At most, they are merely societal outliers. Also, we like to pretend that they chose to become disconnected from the greater mass of society. We do not want to recognize our part in making them that way or shunning them out.

The truth is that most feel the same sense of alienation and emptiness a lot of the time. They just do not act out their inner pain so intensely and destructively because their symptoms are less. The exceptions and outliers are there to teach us an all-important lesson. *"That we must embrace policies of inclusion for all and not just for some."*

(Sharon) In your last earthly tour, you were able to work so many miracles for others, such as healing the lame, restoring sight to the blind and raising Lazarus from the dead? Weren't you interfering with their learning lessons at the time?

(Jesus) No! I was merely accelerating their learning. I realized early the blindness, lameness and all other forms of sickness and suffering were just symptoms and not causes in themselves. The real problem source was the guilt and self-hate within that was then projected to the body in the form of these ailments. As with the Martyr, they were trying to mitigate God's wrath by first inflicting it on themselves. They were ensnared in dreams of shame and deep unworthiness and were, therefore, unable to forgive themselves for some past event. When I forgave them their sins, they finally forgave themselves. Since their inner guilt and unworthiness was no longer there, the symptoms quickly disappeared.

Thus there was never anything physical wrong with their legs or their eyes. They were just psychologically and spiritually sick inside and in great need of spiritual healing. They had self-crippled themselves through guilt, and ultimately it was not my forgiveness, but their own that enabled them to heal. It works much the same as when a Dr. restores and revives a patient from some affliction, through some supposed "*Miracle Cure.*" This is actually just a placebo. The patient has no faith in their individual healing power, but great faith in the Dr. and the "*Miracle Cure*" provided – so it works. They are healed through the projection of their innate healing power to these external proxies.

(Sharon) How about Lazarus, he was already dead!

(Jesus) Lazarus was not dead. Nothing that lives can ever die! He had merely given up his identification with his earthly body, by the time I arrived. Knowing that Lazarus was still very much alive, I was able to communicate to him through the One-Mind and convince him to take up identification with his body, once more. My faith in him worked the miracle. However, I could not have done it without Lazarus's help.

In many ways, raising Lazarus was much more involved than accomplishing my own resurrection, because I also needed his cooperation. He only agreed to come back to help me help others. He was genuinely done with that particular body and life at that point and did not hang out in it much longer after that. His revivification can, therefore, be seen as his last gift. Today you might call this a publicity stunt. A mere spectacle to increase the faith of others. It did help tremendously to strengthen their faith for it taught (and rightly so) that even the illusion of death is powerless over truth.

YOU CAN NEVER BE UNFAIRLY TREATED

(Sharon) Another bone I have to pick with you is your declaration in the Course that we cannot be unfairly treated. This seems to go against all the mainstream evidence. Are those women who are raped at gunpoint not unfairly treated? How about those decapitated by ISIS? Or those mercilessly shot to death at the Pulse nightclub in Orlando? Was honest Abe fairly treated when he got shot in the back of the head by John Wilkes Booth? How about those babies born with heart defects that die soon after? It seems the world abounds with numerous indisputable testaments of those unfairly treated.

(Jesus) Everyone who thinks they are in the relative existence must go through the illusion of death sooner or later. Death helps pressurize you to change your ways and to give up old ego habits. Only those who succeed in reaching Truth beforehand, do not need to go through this illusion, one more time. They know there is no death and this world has always been one of shadows. The causes of apparent death are many. Honestly, is at any better to die slowly from cancer than to die suddenly from a heart attack or gunshot? Of course, some will have their preference. If

each life, one were given an infinite amount of time to accomplish their purpose they would just vacillate and pro-
crastinate to the point of complete boredom. Not the sort
of buoyant folk one would want to have over on a Sunday
to perk oneself up before the Monday morning blues.

You must realize, no one survives their purpose. Honest
Abe's particular life purpose was very apparent. It was to
free the slaves and win the American Civil War. Robert E.
Lee surrendered just a few days before Abe's assassination. Similarly, Mahatma Gandhi was shot but only after
first accomplishing his life purpose. Those killed in Orlando helped bring the universal spotlight on hate-crimes.
Collectively they achieved, what individually they never
could. They helped establish greater unity and inclusion
among us, almost overnight. Children born with heart defects or other ailments can often promote prodigious ad-
vances in Medical Science. Their plight truly humbles us
and causes us to be more painfully aware of our ultimate
vulnerability and limitations apart from God.

Nevertheless, most catastrophic or unnerving events cannot be interpreted in a positive light. They are simply the
unfortunate result of choosing with the ego and adopting
its self-sabotaging decisions and behaviors. The ego is

quick to use its catchphrase of "*I am unfairly treated,*" to justify all its attacks and to implant guilt in others. It likes to catalog all such events so that it can sell you a tale of your victim-hood. Doing so, you will never gain mastery over this world of your perceptions because you are failing to take responsibility for it. Instead, you are choosing to see your situation and the world as external to your mind. An outside force with power over your happiness. However, as I said in the Course:

> **"You cannot be unfairly treated. The belief you are is but another form of the idea you are deprived by someone not yourself. Projection of the cause of sacrifice is at the root of everything perceived to be unfair and not your just deserts."**
>
> [ACIM, T-26.X.3:2-4]

Since the world is a projection of your inner thought processes, both conscious and unconscious, all that seems to happen in it is a direct reflection of your decisions and learning lessons. Sometimes a woman who is raped, needed to learn a valuable lesson in forgiveness. In other cases, the outcome may be a child whom she comes to love. At other times, feeling the pressure of her unconscious guilt or bearing dark thoughts of sinfulness or unworthiness within, she actively calls out for this act of retribution. She may not even be consciously aware of this. At one point, she must have, or the rape could never have happened. In these situations, she is very much behaving like the martyr and exacts this form of vengeance on herself to mitigate the vengefulness she projects to God. Every case is different, but to say anything happens randomly and uncalled-for, is to play into the ego's game of victimization.

Others use the catch-phrase "*I am being unfairly treated*" as a means to project guilt upon the world, in an attempt to purchase innocence for themselves.

> **"Beware of the temptation to perceive yourself unfairly treated. In this view, you seek to find an innocence that is not Theirs, but yours alone and at the cost of someone's else's guilt. Can innocence be purchased by the giving of your guilt to someone else?"**
>
> [ACIM, T-26.X.4:1-3]

The essential understanding is that your innocence can never be purchased. Nor need you bargain for it because it was already divinely guaranteed to you in your Creation. When the ego tempts you into seeking for innocence for yourself alone through the projection of guilt, it is merely selling an illusion of innocence to you. One that hides your true innocence beneath the veil of projected guilt.

THE VICIOUS CYCLE

(Sharon) Since the Relative Existence is unreal, why do so few know and why hasn't it come to an end by now? What keeps us believing life is going to work out here?

(Jesus) The unreal can't come to an end because it has never been. It will seem to remain so long as you continue to cherish it. The few that have recognized its non-substantive nature refused to be lured by its empty gifts. All else fell hook, line, and sinker. The relative came into apparent being with the TMI. This established a vicious cycle into place in which our collective guilt became unconscious. This vicious cycle is particularly insidious and made our situation desperately complicated. It is the only reason why the relative existence continues to play itself out in your mind and thought. Without a doubt, this world never happened. However, the instant Adam thought the TMI; the true present became substituted by an unreal past which consisted of dreams of vengeance and self-completion. The vicious cycle continues to keep this past alive in the present through the mechanism of denial. As a result, most have become totally blinded by their belief in guilt and its copious effects. Not fathoming the full extent

of their blindness and being unaware of the traumatic incident from their past, they are unable to heal themselves.

The dynamics of the vicious cycle are incredibly hypnotizing and hard to escape. So much so that the real roots of
the problem are never exposed and raised to conscious
awareness. Thus, like sleepwalkers, they go trolling about,
taking the relative existence to be real in itself. They never
realize it is but a dream of their own making that has long
since disappeared. In fact millions of years ago. Your position then is somewhat similar to that of veterans who have
had their legs blow off with IEDs, who continuously relive
their past trauma, at the cost of present day reality. Nevertheless, since you abide, as always, in the realm of the
Eternal; you have no real justification for being fearful.
Spacetime can at most represent an hallucination temporarily interposing itself before the Sun of Truth.

There is no indefinite future to come, and the past has never been. To you, the future may still seem open and unde-
termined, but that is because your consciousness has not
become sufficiently expansive to take in the full picture.
You are like the goldfish, which keeps circling over-and-
back in the selfsame bowl. Each time you get to the other
side you are all excited and giggly once again thinking these new appearances are happening for real. I can see all
your future and past and know that it is over. To me, it is

just a static and dead thing. A frozen picture, I placed in my attic long ago. However, to you, it still enthralls and presents some semblance of dynamically occurring. Being hopelessly stuck inside this pop-up storybook life, you keep reliving it out and spinning your wheels. You will never escape it so long as you treasure guilt. Only when you have forgiven all those characters whom you perceive in this picture-book, can you withdraw from this bleak manifold!

Even your process of thought is not at random. All has already been played out, including all your motivations, desires, hatreds, intuitions and epiphanies. All lifeless patterns of inspiration and reflection you will ever have, exist as nothing more than as a spectral interference pattern in the higher-dimensional landscape of the mind. I will now refresh you, on the veracious in the hope that you will finally take it to heart.

> **"The world of time is the world of illusion. What happened long ago seems to be happening now. Choices made long since appear to be open; yet to be made. What has been learned and understood and long ago passed by is looked upon as**

a new thought, a fresh idea, a different approach."

[ACIM, MFT.2.3:1-4]

"Time really, then, goes backward to an instant so ancient that it is beyond all memory, and past even the possibility of remembering. Yet because it is an instant that is relived again and again and still again, it seems to be now."

[ACIM, MFT.2.4:1-2]

In fact, the power of denial is so strong that most never even become remotely aware, that there is something fundamentally wrong with this world. Thinking it is all there is, they suspect nothing is hidden behind the screen. They have lost all sense of intuition and smell. Otherwise, they would have detected long ago, that there is something very odious and foul leaking up from its foundations, as you did. In fact, it is the tenacity by which you sunk your teeth into this that extended an invite for me to speak because I can never communicate through a closed mind.

There is no such thing, like a perpetual motion machine, either in this world or the domain of the human psyche. There is always some triggering cause that perpetuates all the dynamics that follow. There must be some source of fuel or power to keep it all going indefinitely. The relative world is no exception. It too is merely an effect of a cause. However, its cause lies not within itself but arises from the projection booth of your mind. If it had a genuine cause within in, then it would be real.

Whenever you are looking at the relative world, you are merely observing the realm of effects, and this is a plane that reflects the quality of your mental action to precision. As the quality of your thinking evolves, the relative world adjusts in perfect correspondence. This guarantees, you will always continue to learn until you can escape from it. All its concepts will be transmogrified and become more expansive so as to adjust to your inward evolution. Eventually, you will no longer perceive a 3-dimensional world, nor your 3-D body because you will have become capable of more accelerated learning.

This vicious cycle of cause-and-effect, which perpetuates the relative existence, can be summarized into a cycle of *denial-separation-fear-judgment-defensiveness*. This composites the fuel which keeps the thought system of the ego alive and well and empowered in your mind. Not seeing the cycle, for what it is, is the real reason most do not make much progress in any given life.

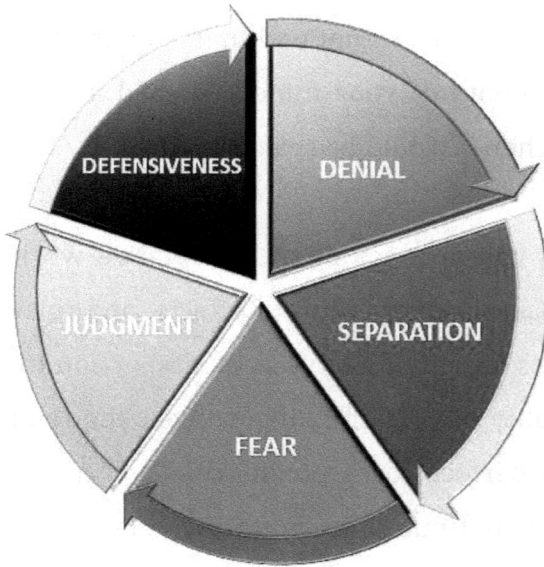

THE CAUSE-AND-EFFECT CYCLE THAT PERPETUATES THE RELATIVE EX-ISTENCE

Denial was what set the whole engine of the world in motion. At this juncture, we had made the decision that maybe we could do better on our own. We wanted to be top dog in our own private show. Hence we set ourselves up to be principal and foremost architect, in our exclusive kingdom and sought complete independence from our Creator. Nonetheless, our dream of specialness was jinxed from the very start because it had no parental consent. Nor was it good for our long term happiness and mental health. We did not fully realize that we could not survive without our Father because, without His seal of approval, nothing real could ever be created. He had put this safety clause into Creation for our protection. It was there to guarantee the Kingdom would never become fragmented and isolated. In many ways, it is similar to the breathalyzer equipment placed in the car of a chronically drunk driver which prevents the car from starting unless one provides a clean blow.

From that moment on, it has been the Tale of the Prodigal Son. We have been wandering ever since, dragging ourselves through the hot deserts and frozen Siberian wastelands of the world, finding all our credit cards maxed out. Our lips forever parched from being unable to taste truth, for far too long. Our zealous attachment to idols and illusions are powerless to quench our real thirst. Our eyes are now covered with cataracts and warts from the endless dust storms we have encountered. Our situation is worsened by our torn feet and weary bones and all those hallucinations that continuously pop up to haunt us. The unconscious guilt we needlessly suffer because of our tiny-mad-idea (TMI) makes us unwilling to go Home.

Were we to fully recognize the hell we created for ourselves through our denial, life would be different. We do not see that this world will always remain illusory and insubstantial or that it is impossible for us to truly separate from God and depart from His Kingdom. Through the dynamic of projection, we now think parts of our mind are independent of us. Thus we see ourselves surrounded by a world of bodies and minds that seem to function autonomously. Feeling isolated and alone, we mistakenly think these bodies are our enemies. Fear meanwhile, has coursed its way deep into our veins and bones, and it has strangled our every breath and hope. We do not realize that "other" minds are part of our greater Identity and critical to our healing. Instead, we treat them as strangers, even as alien life forms. We do not recognize they are aspects of our own Whole-Mind from which we have become severely dissociated.

The next phase in this cause-and-effect cycle must be apparent. For those who feel isolated, disenfranchised and cut off from their only of strength are likely to become very judgmental. Judgment becomes the separate mind's weapon of choice for protecting its personal best interests. For it perceives enemies everywhere, out to steal the little that it has. Nor will it recognize that these "others" are part of its greater Self. Feeling fearful, weak and vulnerable, it soon recognizes the need to form alliances. So it builds special love and hate relationships with other minds and bodies. All of which are carefully chosen because of their unique capacities to strengthen its personal position. Once these relationships fail for any reason, they fast become ignored, shunned and forgotten. Nevertheless, the ego never rests. It is always frantically pacing about, eagerly searching for more "special" people, to fashion into jewels for its crown.

Since judgment teaches these "others" that they are a thing apart, we soon become blinded to our true Source of strength. Becoming profoundly invested in the world of spacetime, dreams, and appearances, we all-but guarantee our real problems can never be resolved. Instead, they remain obscured through countless ego-investments, tricks, devices, and deceptions. An immense screen of complexities, contradictions, and twisted interests arises that makes it difficult for us to see. Hypnotized and fully engaged with our ego's chosen substitutes for salvation, the dream of peace becomes replaced with one of anxiety and strife. So the search for wisdom soon degenerates into one of many convoluted arguments and small-talk. Then inventiveness and ingenuity creep in, as our chosen substitutes for Creation. This is followed by magical beliefs becoming rampant in an effort to promote our dream of self-sufficiency.

Firmly locked into this despairing belief system, the ego continues to propagate the myth of its reality. Everywhere you go, it parades before you lovely witnesses to your guilt. However, the one solution which could completely heal and integrate your mind, you never choose to entertain. Never questioning the very foundation of your guilt, is the very recipe for your damnation. Thus you are likely to become particularly judgmental and damning against all those bodies which seem to have power over you and of all who can steal your piece of the pie. All special hate relationships arise in this void where there is a perceived loss in power.

The last phase of this cause-and-effect cycle becomes the definitive nail in your coffin. For divorced from your authentic Identity, you engage a multiplicity of defenses to protect your vested interests. Having already judged and condemned all, you feel surrounded by enemies. Fear having buried its way deep into your house of flesh, you become unwilling to come out of your shell. Thus you block yourself off from your only real source of healing. Defenses then serve a dual purpose. Firstly they protect the crown jewels you have stolen from "others, " and hide them away securely behind the gates of your pet paradise. Secondly, ego defenses are incorrectly perceived as serving for your protection.

Behind the gates, only your most special friends are ever given access, and these privileges can be revoked at any time. Everyone else is barred from entering your slice of heaven. You may have noticed this for yourself. How people often clam up for no apparent reason, even though you are only engaging them in simple conversation. Their shields are up and their silence and lack of response tell you in no uncertain terms, that you have overstepped an invisible barrier. You may have simply dropped some ice breaking comment, and yet now you feel frozen out and totally perplexed.

Many are overtly afraid of becoming overly familiar with anyone. Afraid to disclose their true thoughts. They believe mind and thought exposure, leaves them vulnerable. They become reluctant to engage any deeper and shut off all doors to their world. Often they have been wounded in the past and have lost all trust. Likewise are they vigilant against all intimacy. Often their defenses are more evident to family and friends than to strangers they will never meet again. Many will not accept kindness and wisdom in forms they do not like.

Defenses serve as the essential protection for the ego's thought because the ego does believe its enemies are powerful and is therefore continuously anxious. It predicts that these rivals may lay siege at any moment and steal back the crown jewels, it has stolen. It projects to its enemies both suspicion and the desire for vengeance. It fully expects retribution for all unjust judgments and attacks it has successfully launched in the past. So does your frightened mind cower behind its vast network of defenses! Each day, it diligently builds up its stockpiles of armor and bastions of self-protection and deploys various psychological defenses.

It squanders all your time in wasteful distractions and nonsensical pursuits while chasing and indulging every vain desire in the hope of winding down the clock. Then it goes about ignoring all alien perspectives and threatening situations that may be upsetting to its fixed personal views. It hopes to be never found out! Nor can it tolerate any silence and meditation. Its anxiety rises asymptotically, anytime you are being silent and still. It will say something hopelessly inane like "*The devil finds work for idle hands."* Yes, it would prefer to be surrounded by a company of idiots and voluptuaries, rather than tolerate its own company for long. Meanwhile, it remains in terror, that one day its meager defenses will be perforated and blown apart. That its enemies will sneak in and gain the advantage, like the Greeks with their Trojan horse. Thus it never picnics out in the open, lest its crown jewels become exposed to "other" nefarious egos. It prefers to remain self-isolated behind the gates of its private world. Over time its nerves become frayed, and it starts to become truly irrational and paranoid. Fearing its private thoughts, it imputes malicious intentions everywhere it goes.

Soon it morphs into an insane fear-poisoned caricature in a dream. Since it projects to God a replica of its own thought, it begins to see Him as a God of vengeance. Nor will it ever let its defenses down, lest it become overrun by enemies. All the same, not letting others in, it cannot heal. Nor can any light ever enter the dark and twisted maze of its self-deceptions. No there is no room left for anything but rats, lice and vermin and more ghoul-like specters, looking very deficient in vitamin D. Eventually the ego perceives the impossibility of its situation. It is then that you feel its death-wish creeping into your mind and thought. So does it coerce you into becoming a willing sacrifice to its god of death, once more!

THE FINAL PICTURE

This discourse had been a tremendous inspiration. I had finally received some deep and revealing answers to questions that had puzzled me almost forever. J. had taught how unconscious guilt underpinned the world and the perfect applicability of quantum forgiveness to heal and release us. It was all beginning to add up. The ego had always been just a phantom formed in the dim haze of our guilt thoughts. One incessantly yelling out for more attacks and condemnations and eager to sell us on sin. Yes, this world had always been just our personal picture of Dorian Gray staring back into our face. However, I had one more question that still needed answering, and so I put it forward.

(Sharon) It seems we made just one relatively innocuous mistake and this led to our futile wandering in a nowhere land, for millions of years. It is as if we were playing chess in five dimensions and accidentally moved our pawn into the wrong position, hoping this minor indiscretion would be overlooked. Instead, before we could catch our breath, it was instantly checkmate, and we were booted out the door of the Kingdom.

(Jesus) Yes, you have always been a shoddy chess-player Sharon, or you would have known there are no accidental moves in chess. Merely good and strategic maneuvers or else thoughtless ones. Used wisely the pawn can be as powerful as any other piece on the board, as many grandmasters can tell you to their profound regret. From the very beginning, I have said the TMI was an unreal thought, and yet you have continuously ignored this and played it down. All effects arising from it are therefore powerless and inconsequential. Your one mistake is continuing to take them very seriously, and this places you in two very opposed states of mind. It is a central mistake to make illusions or any source of darkness real, rather than applying the remedy that has been given. Likewise, you believe the world is happening now. Thus you insist on attempting to solve problems, which do not exist. It has always been simply a case of just one problem and one solution. Forgiveness is the counter-dream to replace all beliefs in guilt. It is this that will wake you up from all terrifying dreams of your ego and heal you in the end. Meanwhile, the Holy Spirit is here to guide and restore your mind back to sanity.

(Sharon) Since the Son retains an eternal free will, isn't it possible for us to think the TMI all over again? That is, once we are all safely restored to the Kingdom?

(Jesus) I was hoping you wouldn't ask that. I steered well away from answering this in the Course. My one goal was to teach how you can remove all obstacles to healing, not to establish new ones. My aim is to have you identify and expose that false voice within, that continuously preaches of your guilt.

Yes, we as the Son, were given eternal free will. Hence we can always think and do as we wish! All the same, just because something is possible doesn't make it probable. I have already related how God Created the Holy Spirit after the TMI to restore our Mind back to sanity. This Voice will remain to reinforce our sane thinking and choosing, even when we all have been fully healed. It will always be here, to gently remind us that it is indeed impossible to rule in any real Kingdom apart from God.

For the TMI to happen again, the entire Sonship would have to lose its collective sanity, all at once, even with the guidance of the Holy Spirit. How likely is this to happen?

Remember I learned how to uproot and heal our original mistake even when mired deep in the pits of darkness. Then there are all those Enlightened Masters, who share the One-Mind with us. They are also here to help. Besides, ever since Adam tasted that apple laced with cyanide, he has been throwing up wickedly in that eternal Garden. I sincerely doubt he will be tempted to imbibe that apple ever again.

TINY MAD IDEA

The Relative World Belief - I

Copyright © 2016 Sharon Moriarty

ISBN (Print) : 978-0-9971179-4-3

Library Of Congress Control Number : 2016915439

GATEWAY TO ETERNITY PUBLICATIONS

http://www.GatewayToEternity.com

Other Books by Sharon Moriarty

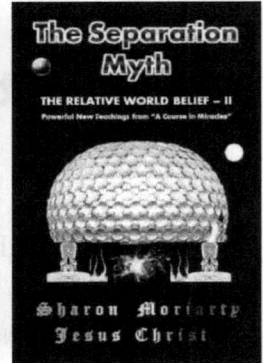

Available now on Amazon and CreateSpace

http://www.amazon.com